Algebra 1
Common Core

Common Core Standards Practice and Review

Progress Monitoring Assessments

D1296009

PEARSON

Boston, Massachusetts   Chandler, Arizona   Glenview, Illinois   Upper Saddle River, New Jersey

Table of Contents

Summative Assessments, Form K

Common Core End-of-Course Assessment 95

Common Core Performance-Based Assessment

SAT/ACT Preparation

Common Core Standards Practice Answers A1

Answers A8

Common Core Performance-Based Assessment

Scoring Rubrics A16

SAT/ACT Practice Test Answers A20

Student Answer Sheets

To the Teacher

Pearson is pleased to offer you *Common Core Standards Practice and Review • Progress Monitoring Assessments*, a comprehensive resource of assessments that you can use to monitor your students' progress throughout the school year and to help them prepare for high-stakes Common Core assessments. These assessments can be used to inform instruction (formative) or to evaluate student learning (summative).

Screening Test

Before launching into the curriculum, you may want to gather information on how proficient your students are with the prerequisite concepts and skills that will allow them to be successful in the course. Use the Screening Test to measure your students' readiness for this course. The Screening Test Report, which lists all of the skills assessed on the test, can be used to isolate areas of weakness students may have.

Common Core Standards Practice and Teacher Notes

Starting on page 1, these 30 pages offer students weekly practice on targeted Common Core Standards. The assessment items follow the progression of concepts and skills found in Pearson's *Algebra 1 Common Core* and focus in particular on the standards that are considered major content emphases. Students will encounter assessment items that are representative of the kinds of items they will find on the upcoming assessments from the Partnership for the Assessment of Readiness for College and Career (PARCC) and Smarter Balanced Assessment Consortium (SBAC). Each weekly practice has a Teacher Notes page that helps you see how to use the practice page in class. The notes will include correlation to Common Core State Standards and Mathematical Practices.

Common Core Readiness Assessments

Each of the five (5) Common Core Readiness Assessments focuses on the concepts and skills that students are expected to master in 2-, or 3-chapter increments. The Common Core Readiness Assessment Reports, found after each Common Core Readiness Assessment, identify the standard(s) that each item assesses and provides lesson references where students can gain more practice with the concept or skill, as needed.

Summative Assessments

These assessments can be used to evaluate student learning at specified intervals. There are four (4) Quarter Tests, a Mid-Course Test, and a cumulative Final Test. All of these are available at two levels, G and K. The Form G tests are designed to measure students' mastery of content with the rigor presented in the lessons and exercises of the Student Edition while the Form K tests assess the same content, but are more appropriate for less proficient readers, English Language Learners (ELLs), and struggling students.

End-of-Course Assessment

The End-of-Course Assessment provides practice for the Common Core End-of-Course Assessments currently under development by the two assessment consortia, PARCC and SBAC. Students will encounter innovative assessment items. The assessment items focus on the major content emphases of both PARCC and SBAC assessments, while still including assessment of the supporting and additional content emphases. The End-of-Course Report can be used to evaluate students' mastery of these content emphases and to identify areas of potential weakness on the high-stakes assessments.

Performance-Based Assessments

The four (4) Performance-Based Assessments offer students rich and complex, multi-part, real-world tasks to help them prepare for the Performance-Based Assessment or Performance Tasks that they will be expected to complete as part of the PARCC or SBAC assessment. In the Answers section, you will find a scoring rubric to evaluate student work on these tasks.

SAT and ACT Practice

These pages can acquaint students with topics and question formats that they are likely to find on the SAT or ACT. The information provided on pages 115 through 121 can help students feel less anxious when they take these high-stakes assessments, and the practice test provides them with familiarity about the format and content of the assessment items.

Screening Test

Choose the best answer for the problems.

1. Which of the following statements about irrational numbers is true?

   A All irrational numbers are divisible by more than two integers.

   B All irrational numbers are divisible by exactly two integers.

   C All irrational numbers have terminating decimals that do not repeat.

   D All irrational numbers have decimals that do not terminate or repeat.

2. Which of the following is an irrational number?

   F 3

   G $0.\overline{3}$

   H $\sqrt{3}$

   J $\dfrac{1}{3}$

3. Which is the best approximation for $\sqrt{5}$?

   A 2.1

   B 2.2

   C 2.3

   D 2.5

4. Which number is closest to $\sqrt{2}$?

   F 0.4

   G 1

   H 1.4

   J 1.5

5. Which numerical expression is equivalent to $7^5 \cdot 7^{-3}$?

   A 49^2

   B 7^2

   C $\dfrac{1}{7^2}$

   D 49^{-15}

6. Which of the following is equivalent to $5^3 \cdot 5^{-5}$?

   F 25^{-15}

   G -10

   H 25^{-2}

   J $\dfrac{1}{25}$

7. Which is equivalent to $\sqrt{16}$?

   A 4

   B 8

   C 14

   D 32

8. Which of the following is a solution to $x^3 = 8$?

   F 24

   G 5

   H $2.7\overline{3}$

   J 2

9. The estimated population of Fiji in 2012 was about 9×10^5. The estimated population of Gibraltar in the same year was about 3×10^4. About how many times greater was the population of Fiji than Gibraltar?

   A 3 times greater

   B 10 times greater

   C 30 times greater

   D 300 times greater

10. A species of phytoplankton measures about 2×10^{-6} in. A grain of sand measures about 1×10^{-4} in. About how many times longer is the grain of sand than the phytoplankton?

    F 20 times greater

    G 50 times greater

    H 100 times greater

    J 200 times greater

11. Earth is about 9.3×10^7 mi from the Sun. Saturn is about 8.9×10^8 mi from the Sun. About how much further from the Sun is Saturn than Earth?

    A 7.97×10^8 mi
    B 9.6×10^0 mi
    C 4.0×10^7 mi
    D 4.0×10^8 mi

12. What is the sum of 3.6×10^{-2} and 2.4×10^3?

    F 6.0×10^5
    G 6.0×10^1
    H 2.436×10^1
    J 2.40036×10^3

13. What is the unit rate in miles per minute as shown in the graph?

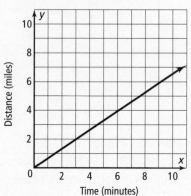

    A $\dfrac{2 \text{ mi}}{3 \text{ min}}$

    B $\dfrac{3 \text{ mi}}{2 \text{ min}}$

    C $\dfrac{0.6 \text{ mi}}{6 \text{ min}}$

    D 1.5 mi/min

14. The speed of Car A is shown in the graph. The speed of Car B is shown in the table. Which Car is traveling at the greater speed?

Car A

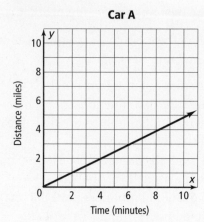

Car B	
Distance (mi)	Time (hr)
75	3
150	6
225	9
300	12

    F Car A
    G Car B
    H Both cars are traveling at the same rate.

15. Which is the slope of the line?

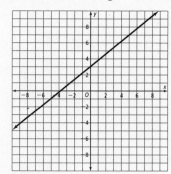

    A $\dfrac{3}{4}$

    B $\dfrac{4}{3}$

    C 3

    D 4

16. What is the equation of the line?

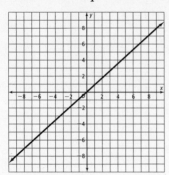

F $y = -\dfrac{9}{10}x$

G $y = -\dfrac{10}{9}x$

H $y = \dfrac{9}{10}x$

J $y = \dfrac{10}{9}x$

17. Which of the following statements is true?
$$8 - (7 - 6x) = 9x - (4 + 3x)$$

A The equation has one solution.

B The equation has an infinite number of solutions.

C The equation has no solution.

D The equation has two solutions.

18. Solve the equation for n.
$$-7(n - 2) + 2n(15 - 8) = 6(2n + 4)$$

F $n = -2$

G $n = 15.2$

H $n = -7.6$

J $n = -11$

19. Line a passes through points $(0, 4)$ and $(1, 7)$. Line b passes through points $(2, 1)$ and $(6, 4)$. Which of the following statements is true?

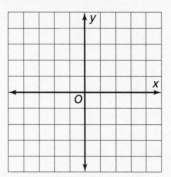

A Lines a and b intersect at point $(0, 0)$.

B Lines a and b intersect at point $(-2, -2)$.

C Lines a and b intersect at point $\left(3, \dfrac{3}{4}\right)$.

D Lines a and b do not intersect.

20. At which point do the two lines intersect?
$$\begin{cases} 2x + y = 8 \\ y = -3(x - 3) \end{cases}$$

F $(0, 8)$

G $(3, -2)$

H $(2, 4)$

J $(1, 6)$

21. Which table does NOT represent a function?

A

x	y
1	1
2	1
3	2
4	2

B

x	y
2	3
1	1
0	0
−1	1

C

x	y
1	1
1	2
2	3
2	4

D

x	y
−1	−3
0	−2
1	−1
2	6

22. Karen sells tickets at a movie theater. Last night she sold 128 tickets for a total of $1108. Adult's tickets cost $10 and children's tickets cost $6. How many of each kind of ticket did Karen sell?

F 22 adult's tickets, 106 children's tickets
G 43 adult's tickets, 85 children's tickets
H 64 adult's tickets, 64 children's tickets
J 85 adult's tickets, 43 children's tickets

23. Which function has the greater slope?

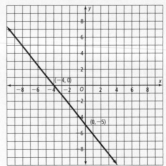

x	y
4	7
2	2
0	−3
−2	−8

A The function of the graph has the greater slope.
B The function of the table has the greater slope.
C Both of the functions have the same slope.
D The function of the table has a slope that is greater in parts and less in other parts of the function.

24. Which of the following describes a linear function?

F $3(x + 2y) − 4 = x + 5y$
G $ax^2 + bx + c = 0$
H $(a + b)^2$
J $A = \pi r^2$

25. For 12 months, Jeanne has belonged to a book-of-the-month club. Jeanne has spent $70.45 on the club. The first month, she paid the monthly fee and spent an additional $10.45 on books. She has only paid the monthly fee since then. What are the initial value and the rate of change of this function?

A initial value: 5; rate of change: 10.45
B initial value: 10.45; rate of change: 60
C initial value: 10.45; rate of change: 5
D initial value: 15.45; rate of change: 70.45

26. Which statement about the graph is true?

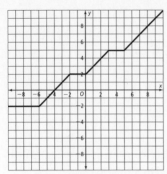

   F The graph is linear and increasing.
   G The graph is linear and decreasing.
   H The graph is nonlinear and increasing.
   J The graph is nonlinear and decreasing.

27. Which transformation maps figure *ABCDEF* to figure *A'B'C'D'E'F'*?

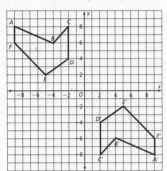

   A rotation
   B reflection
   C translation
   D dilation

28. Which must be true for two figures to be congruent?

   F The two figures must be a reflection of one another.
   G The two figures must have the same orientation.
   H The two figures must lie in the same plane.
   J The two figures must have the same size and shape.

29. What would be the coordinates of the image of $\triangle ABC$ after a dilation with the scale factor 2 about the origin?

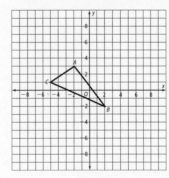

   A $A'(-2, 3), B'(2, -3), C'(-5, 1)$
   B $A'(-4, 5), B'(4, -5), C'(-7, 3)$
   C $A'(-4, 6), B'(4, -6), C'(-10, 2)$
   D $A'(-1, 1.5), B'(1, -1.5), C'(-2.5, 0.05)$

30. Figure *A* is similar to figure *A'*. Which pair of terms describes how to transform figure *A* to figure *A'*?

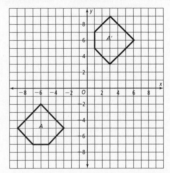

   F translation and reflection
   G dilation and rotation
   H rotation and translation
   J dilation and translation

31. Given $\ell_1 \| \ell_2$ and cut by transversal ℓ_3, which statement is true?

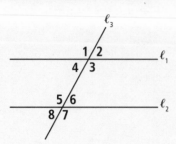

A $m\angle 2 + m\angle 3 = 180°$ and $\angle 2 \cong \angle 6$, so $m\angle 3 + m\angle 6 = 180°$

B $m\angle 5 + m\angle 8 = 180°$ and $\angle 6 \cong \angle 7$, so $m\angle 6 + m\angle 8 = 180°$

C $\angle 5 \cong \angle 7$ and $\angle 5 \cong \angle 4$, so $\angle 7 \cong \angle 4$

D $\angle 1 \cong \angle 2$ and $\angle 1 \cong \angle 5$, so $\angle 2 \cong \angle 5$

32. A 30 ft cable extends from the floor of the lookout of a fire tower. The cable is anchored to the ground 18 ft away from the base of the tower. What is the height of the floor of the lookout tower?

F 48 ft

G 35 ft

H 24 ft

J 10 ft

33. What is the distance between points A and B?

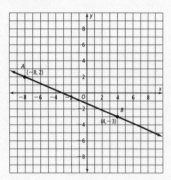

A 7   **C** 15

B 13   **D** 17

34. A cylinder has a height of 7 in. and a diameter of 6 in. What is the volume of the cylinder to the nearest cubic inch?

F $V = 66$ in.^{3}

G $V = 132$ in.^{3}

H $V = 198$ in.^{3}

J $V = 792$ in.^{3}

35. Which of the following best describes the relationship of the data?

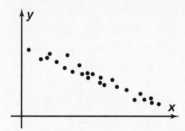

A strong positive correlation

B strong negative correlation

C weak positive correlation

D weak negative correlation

36. The equation for the line of best fit relating the weight of a child in kilograms y in relation to the child's age in years x. Which of the following statements is true?

$$y = 3x + 3.25$$

F The average weight in kilograms is 3 times the age.

G The average weight in kilograms is 3 times the height.

H The average child is 3 years old.

J The average child weighed 3.25 kg at birth.

37. The table shows students' average test scores in relation to their average study times. What conclusion could you draw from the data?

Test Score	Study Time (minutes)				
	At least 60	45–59	30–44	15–29	0–14
A	20	15	13	6	3
B	10	18	14	10	4
C	5	9	21	19	13
D	2	5	10	12	25
F	0	1	2	4	8

A There is a positive correlation between study time and test scores.
B There is a negative correlation between study time and test scores.
C There is an inverse correlation between study time and test scores.
D There is no correlation between study time and test scores.

Screening Test Report

CCSS Standards	Test Item(s)	Proficient? Yes or No?
Know That There Are Numbers That Are Not Rational, and Approximate Them by Rational Numbers.		
8.NS.1 Understand informally that every number has a decimal expansion; the rational numbers are those with decimal expansions that terminate in 0s or eventually repeat. Know that other numbers are called irrational.	1, 2	
8.NS.2 Use rational approximations of irrational numbers to compare the size of irrational numbers, locate them approximately on a number line diagram, and estimate the value of expressions.	3, 4	
Work with Radicals and Integer Exponents		
8.EE.1 Know and apply the properties of integer exponents to generate equivalent numerical expressions.	5, 6	
8.EE.2 Use square root and cube root symbols to represent solutions to equations of the form $x2 = p$ and $x3 = p$, where p is a positive rational number. Evaluate square roots of small perfect squares and cube roots of small perfect cubes. Know that $\sqrt{2}$ is irrational.	7, 8	
8.EE.3 Use numbers expressed in the form of a single digit times an integer power of 10 to estimate very large or very small quantities, and to express how many times as much one is than the other.	9, 10	
8.EE.4 Perform operations with numbers expressed in scientific notation, including problems where both decimal and scientific notation are used. Use scientific notation and choose units of appropriate size for measurements of very large or very small quantities (e.g., use millimeters per year for seafloor spreading). Interpret scientific notation that has been generated by technology.	11, 12	
Understand the Connections Between Proportional Relationships, Lines, and Linear Relationships.		
8.EE.5 Graph proportional relationships, interpreting the unit rate as the slope of the graph. Compare two different proportional relationships represented in different ways.	13, 14	
8.EE.6 Use similar triangles to explain why the slope m is the same between any two distinct points on a non-vertical line in the coordinate plane; derive the equation $y = mx$ for a line through the origin and the equation $y = mx + b$ for a line intercepting the vertical axis at b.	15, 16	
Analyze and Solve Linear Equations and Pairs of Simultaneous Linear Equations.		
8.EE.7.a Solve linear equations in one variable. Give examples of linear equations in one variable with one solution, infinitely many solutions, or no solutions. Show which of these possibilities is the case by successively transforming the given equation into simpler forms, until an equivalent equation of the form $x = a$, $a = a$, or $a = b$ results (where a and b are different numbers).	17	

CCSS Standards	Test Item(s)	Proficient? Yes or No?
8.EE.7.b Solve linear equations in one variable. Solve linear equations with rational number coefficients, including equations whose solutions require expanding expressions using the distributive property and collecting like terms.	18	
8.EE.8.a Analyze and solve pairs of simultaneous linear equations in two variables correspond to points of intersection of their graphs, because points of intersection satisfy both equations simultaneously.	19	
8.EE.8.b Analyze and solve pairs of simultaneous linear equations. Solve systems of two linear equations in two variables algebraically, and estimate solutions by graphing the equations. Solve simple cases by inspection.	20	
8.EE.8.c Analyze and solve pairs of simultaneous linear equations. Solve real-world and mathematical problems leading to two linear equations in two variables.	22	
Define, Evaluate, and Compare Functions.		
8.F.1 Understand that a function is a rule that assigns to each input exactly one output. The graph of a function is the set of ordered pairs consisting of an input and the corresponding output.	21	
8.F.2 Compare properties of two functions each represented in a different way (algebraically, graphically, numerically in tables, or by verbal descriptions).	23	
8.F.3 Interpret the equation $y = mx + b$ as defining a linear function, whose graph is a straight line; give examples of functions that are not linear.	24	
Use Functions to Model Relationships Between Quantities.		
8.F.4 Construct a function to model a linear relationship between two quantities. Determine the rate of change and initial value of the function from a description of a relationship or from two (x, y) values, including reading these from a table or from a graph. Interpret the rate of change and initial value of a linear function in terms of the situation it models, and in terms of its graph or a table of values.	25	
8.F.5 Describe qualitatively the functional relationship between two quantities by analyzing a graph (e.g., where the function is increasing or decreasing, linear or nonlinear). Sketch a graph that exhibits the qualitative features of a function that has been described verbally.	26	
Understand Congruence and Similarity Using Physical Models, Transparences, or Geometry Software.		
8.G.1.a Verify experimentally the properties of rotations, reflections, and translations:. Lines are taken to lines, and line segments to line segments of the same length.	27	
8.G.2 Understand that a two-dimensional figure is congruent to another if the second can be obtained from the first by a sequence of rotations, reflections, and translations; given two congruent figures, describe a sequence that exhibits the congruence between them.	28	
8.G.3 Describe the effect of dilations, translations, rotations, and reflections on two-dimensional figures using coordinates.	29	
8.G.4 Understand that a two-dimensional figure is similar to another if the second can be obtained from the first by a sequence of rotations, reflections, translations, and dilations; given two similar two dimensional figures, describe a sequence that exhibits the similarity between them.	30	
8.G.5 Use informal arguments to establish facts about the angle sum and exterior angle of triangles, about the angles created when parallel lines are cut by a transversal, and the angle-angle criterion for similarity of triangles.	31	

CCSS Standards	Test Item(s)	Proficient? Yes or No?
Understand and Apply the Pythagorean Theorem.		
8.G.7 Apply the Pythagorean Theorem to determine unknown side lengths in right triangles in real-world and mathematical problems in two and three dimensions.	32	
8.G.8 Apply the Pythagorean Theorem to find the distance between two points in a coordinate system.	33	
Solve Real-World and Mathematical Problems Involving Volume of Cylinders, Cones, and Spheres.		
8.G.9 Know the formulas for the volumes of cones, cylinders, and spheres and use them to solve real-world and mathematical problems.	34	
Investigate Patterns of Association in Bivariate Data.		
8.SP.1 Construct and interpret scatter plots for bivariate measurement data to investigate patterns of association between two quantities. Describe patterns such as clustering, outliers, positive or negative association, linear association, and nonlinear association.	35	
8.SP.3 Use the equation of a linear model to solve problems in the context of bivariate measurement data, interpreting the slope and intercept.	36	
8.SP.4 Understand that patterns of association can also be seen in bivariate categorical data by displaying frequencies and relative frequencies in a two-way table. Construct and interpret a two-way table summarizing data on two categorical variables collected from the same subjects. Use relative frequencies calculated for rows or columns to describe possible association between the two variables.	37	

Student Comments:

_____

_____

_____

_____

Parent Comments:

_____

_____

_____

_____

Teacher Comments:

_____

_____

_____

_____

Algebra 1
Common Core

Weekly Practice
Overview

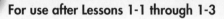

OVERVIEW

Looking Back	Mathematics of the Week	Looking Ahead
In Grade 7, students used variables to represent quantities in real-world situations (7.EE.B.4.a). In Grade 8, students used variables to represent function situations (8.F.B.4).	Students write and evaluate algebraic expressions. They also simplify numerical and algebraic expressions containing exponents and develop an understanding of irrational numbers.	In Chapter 2, students use variables to solve equations (A.REI.B.3). In Chapter 8, students will add, subtract, multiply, and factor polynomials (A.APR.A.1, A.SSE.A.2).

COMMON CORE CONTENT STANDARDS

N.RN.B.3 Explain why the sum or product of two rational numbers is rational; that the sum of a rational number and an irrational number is irrational; …

A.SSE.A.1.a Interpret parts of an expression, such as terms, factors, and coefficients.

A.SSE.A.2 Use the structure of an expression to identify ways to rewrite it.

Common Core Mathematical Practice Standards: 1, 2, 4, 6, 7
Materials: Calculator

TEACHING NOTES

Selected Response

1. *Error Analysis*: Students show understanding of foundational mathematical concepts and vocabulary. They should know that the given expression has three terms. If the student selects answer B, he or she may think that the first coefficient indicates the number of terms. If the student selects answers C or D, the student is guessing and does not understand the definition of "term." Review as needed the meaning of key vocabulary.

2. *Error Analysis*: Students must interpret each term in the expression as they work to find the unit cost for hitting baseballs. Students should realize that the term $0.15b$ represents the cost per baseball and the term 5 represents the $5 the complex charges to use the facility. If the student selects answer A, he or she likely failed to separate the two costs. If the student selects answer B, the student may not understand the parts of the expression. If the student selects answer D, the student does not understand how to find the cost per baseball by analyzing the expression.

Constructed Response

3. Students are expected to rewrite the expression, substituting 3 for a and 5 for b, and then evaluate the expression. Check that students have rewritten each term in the expression accurately. Students may benefit from using a calculator to find 15^3.

Extended Response

4. Students are asked to critique the reasoning of a student as they explain operations with real numbers. Check that students understand what real numbers are. They should be encouraged to show multiple examples: one with two rational numbers, one with a rational and an irrational number, and one with two irrational numbers.

Common Core Standards Practice

Week 1

Selected Response

1. How many terms are in the expression $4a + a^2 + 6a^3$?

A 3

B 4

C 5

D 7

2. A sporting complex charges \$5 to use its facility. The expression $0.15b + 5$ models the total cost to hit b baseballs in the batting cages. What is the cost per baseball?

A \$5.15

B \$5.00

C \$0.15

D \$0.10

Constructed Response

3. What is the value of the expression $2(ab)^3 - 3a + 5b$ for $a = 3$ and $b = 5$?

Extended Response

4. A student stated that the sum of two real numbers is always an integer. Is the student correct? Explain why or why not and provide an example to support your answer.

OVERVIEW

Looking Back	Mathematics of the Week	Looking Ahead
In Chapter 1, students developed an understanding for using variables and for evaluating expressions containing variables, including using the Distributive Property expand expressions and to combine like terms (6.EE.A.2.a, 6.EE.A.2.c, 6.EE.A.3, 7.EE.B.4.a).	Students solve equations using mental math and using tables. They also make tables for real-world situations, write two-variable equations based on tables, and graph the data from the tables in the first quadrant of the coordinate plane.	In Chapter 2, students will solve equations using Properties of Equality (A.REI.B.3). In Chapter 5, students will develop a deeper understanding of two-variable equations as linear functions (F.IE.B.4).

COMMON CORE MATHEMATICAL CONTENT STANDARDS

A.CED.A.1 Create equations and inequalities in one variable and use them to solve problems.

A.CED.A.2 Create equations in two or more variables to represent relationships between quantities; graph equations on coordinate axes with labels and scales.

Common Core Mathematical Practice Standards: 1, 2, 3, 4, 6, 7

TEACHING NOTES

Selected Response

1. *Error Analysis*: Students write an equation to match a written expression. They should be able to translate from verbal to algebraic forms. If the student selects answers B or C, the student does not understand the meaning of the term "sum." If the student selects answer D, the student is transposing 9 and 17 in the original statement.

2. *Error Analysis*: Students are expected to determine a solution to the equation given. If the student answers A, he or she is not solving correctly. If the student answers B or D, the student is likely substituting the first number of the ordered pair as y and the second number of the ordered pair as x.

Constructed Response

3. Students are representing a relationship between two variable using tables and equations. For part (a), verify that students see that the relationship between the two variables remains the same with both forms. As needed, ask students to explain each set of value in their tables: "If Allie works ___hours, she earns ___." For part (b), students extend the table in part (a) to confirm that the relationship between the two variables remains constant.

Extended Response

4. Students represent the relationship between values in three ways and consider situations that can be modeled by a linear relationship. For part (a), remind students to use the header x for the top of the first column and the header y for the top of the second column. For part (b), ask students to identify the multiplier of the variable (5), and ask what is added to the product (55). Students use these to write the equation. For part (c), have students mark the first line above the x-axis as 55. For part (d), remind students that the situation they develop should have a constant, 55, and 5 as a multiplier of x.

Common Core Standards Practice

Week 2

Selected Response

1. Which equation represents the following sentence?

   The sum of a number n and 9 is 17.

   A $n + 9 = 17$
   B $9n = 17$
   C $n - 9 = 17$
   D $n + 17 = 9$

2. Which ordered pair is a solution to the equation $y = 2x + 8$?

   A $(2, 1)$
   B $(-2, -3)$
   C $(0, 8)$
   D $(8, 0)$

Constructed Response

3. Allie earns $5 per hour doing chores.

   a. Make a table and write an equation to show the relationship between the number of hours worked h and the wages earned w.

   b. How many hours will Allie need to work to earn $25?

Extended Response

4. Consider the ordered pairs $(0, 55)$, $(1, 60)$, $(2, 65)$, $(3, 70)$, $(4, 75)$, and $(5, 80)$.

   a. Represent the ordered pairs as a table.

   b. Represent the ordered pairs as an equation.

   c. Represent the ordered pairs as a graph.

   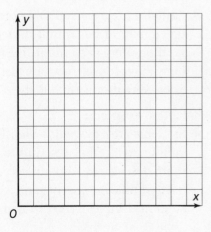

   d. Describe a situation that ordered pairs might represent.

OVERVIEW

Looking Back	Mathematics of the Week	Looking Ahead
In Chapter 1, students used variables to build expressions and equations and evaluated expressions for given values of the variables (A.CED.A.1). Students solved equations using mental math and tables (7.EE.B.4.a, 8.EE.C.7.a).	Students solve equations using Properties of Equality. Starting with one-step equations and then two-step equations, students expand to multi-step equations requiring them to use the Distributive Property.	In this chapter, students will solve equations with variables on both sides (A.CED.A.1) and literal equations (A.CED.A.4). In Chapter 6, they will use solve systems of equations (A.REI.C.6).

COMMON CORE CONTENT STANDARDS

A.CED.A.1 Create equations and inequalities in one variable and use them to solve problems.

A.REI.A.1 Explain each step in solving a simple equation as following from the equality of numbers asserted at the previous step, ...

A.REI.B.3 Solve linear equations and inequalities in one variable, including equations with coefficients represented by letters.

Mathematical Practice Standards: 1, 2, 3, 4, 7, 8
Materials: Calculator

TEACHING NOTES

Selected Response

1. *Error Analysis*: Students solve linear equations in one variable. If a student selects answer B, he or she likely divided rather than multiplying. If the student selects answer C, the student probably divided *and* made a sign error. If the student selects answers D, the student correctly multiplied, but made a sign error.

2. *Error Analysis*: Students are expected to write an equation that models the situation given, and then solve that equation. If a student selects answers A, C, or D, he or she did not set up the equation correctly.

Constructed Response

3. Students are expected to write an equation that models the situation given, and then solve that equation. Verify that students have accounted for all three angles in their equations. Remind them to combine like terms and to add the constants before they solve. Once students have found the value of x, ask if this number is the measure of any of the angles (no). Make sure they complete the task by finding the measure of each angle.

Extended Response

4. Students are expected to identify each step in the solution process by relating the mathematics to a verbal description. If students struggle to identify the appropriate step, have them describe the difference(s) from one equation to the next. If a student continues to have trouble, be specific and ask which step uses the each of the justifications until the student completes the problem.

Common Core Standards Practice   Week 3

Selected Response

1. What is the solution of $-36 = \dfrac{q}{4}$?

    A -144

    B -9

    C 9

    D 144

2. You are buying snacks. You buy 4 apples and a juice. The juice costs $1.75. The total cost is $4.75. How much is 1 apple?

    A $.50

    B $.75

    C $1.00

    D $1.25

Constructed Response

3. The sum of the angle measures of a triangle is 180°. Find the measure of each angle.

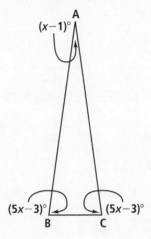

Extended Response

4. Write the correct explanation next to each step.

- Distributive Property
- Simplify using addition.
- Add 5 to each side and simplify.
- Use multiplication to simplify.
- Multiply each side by $-\dfrac{5}{2}$ and simplify.

Steps	Explanation
$-\dfrac{2}{5}(x + 5) - 3 = 65$	Original equation
$-\dfrac{2}{5}(x) - \dfrac{2}{5}(5) - 3 = 65$	_____
$-\dfrac{2}{5}(x) + (-2) - 3 = 65$	_____
$-\dfrac{2}{5}x - 5 = 65$	_____
$-\dfrac{2}{5}x = 70$	_____
$x = -175$	_____

OVERVIEW

Looking Back	Mathematics of the Week	Looking Ahead
Earlier in Chapter 2, students wrote and solved equations using the Properties of Equality (8.EE.C.7.b, A.CED.A.1, A.REI.B.3).	Students solve literal equations for a variable and solve equations with variables on both sides.	In Chapter 6, students use solve systems of equations (A.REI.C.6). In Chapter 9, students extend their understanding of solving one-variable equations to solving quadratic equations (A.CED.A.1).

COMMON CORE CONTENT STANDARDS

A.CED.A.1 Create equations and inequalities in one variable and use them to solve problems.

A.CED.A.4 Rearrange formulas to highlight a quantity of interest, using the same reasoning as in solving equations.

A.REI.B.3 Solve linear equations and inequalities in one variable, including equations with coefficients represented by letters.

> **Mathematical Practice Standards:** 1, 2, 4, 7
> **Materials:** Calculator

TEACHING NOTES

Selected Response

1. *Error Analysis*: Students rewrite an equation in a given form. If a student answers A or B, he or she did not use the Division Property of Equality to divide each side of the equation by RT in order to isolate n. If the student answers D, it is possible that the student started to use the Division Property of Equality and was distracted and did not complete the problem.

Constructed Response

2. Students solve a linear equation with two given values. Ask students to write the original equation and then substitute the values for F and a. Recommend that they circle m for mass so that they do not confuse the variable for the m that represents meter. Ask students to indicate which units are on both sides of the equation and ask whether these will cancel, requiring students to justify their answers. Recommend that students use a calculator to check the answer.

Extended Response

3. Students write and solve an equation to answer a word problem. Confirm that the students know the meaning of profit and apply the meaning to this situation. Have them write an expression for the profit for a store on Main Street and an expression for the profit for a store on Broad Street. Confirm with students that to find the answer, these expressions must be set equal. For part (b), ask students what they must do to solve the equation. Recommend that students use a calculator to check the answer in the original equation.

Common Core Standards Practice   Week 4

Selected Response

1. Solve the formula $pV = nRT$ for n.

A $n = pV - RT$

B $n = pVRT$

C $n = \dfrac{pV}{RT}$

D $n = pV$

Constructed Response

2. You can find the net force F on an object by using the formula $F = ma$, where m is the mass of the object in kilograms and a is its acceleration in meters per second squared. What is the mass of an object that has a net force of 65 kg m/s^2 and an acceleration of 5 m/s^2?

Extended Response

3. A T-shirt maker wants to open his first store. If he chooses the store on Main Street, he will pay $640 in rent and will charge $30 per T-shirt. If he chooses the store on Broad Street, he will pay $450 in rent and will charge $25 per T-shirt. How many T-shirts would he have to sell in 1 month to make the same profit at either location?

a. Write an equation to solve the problem.

b. Solve the equation you wrote in part (a) to answer the question.

Common Core Standards Practice

OVERVIEW

Looking Back	Mathematics of the Week	Looking Ahead
Earlier in Chapter 2, students wrote and solved equations using the Properties of Equality, building from simple one-step equations to more complicated equations (A.REI.B.3, A.CED.A.1).	Students write and solve special types of equations—proportions. Students apply their understanding of writing proportions to many real-world applications from similar figures.	In Chapter 5, students use proportional thinking to understand rate of change (F.LE.A.1.b) and to write and graph equations for direct variations (A.CED.A.2).

COMMON CORE CONTENT STANDARDS

N.Q.A.1 Use units…to guide the solution of multi-step problems;…choose and interpret the scale and the origin in graphs and data displays.

N.Q.A.3 Choose a level of accuracy appropriate to limitations on measurement…

A.CED.A.1 Create equations and inequalities in one variable and use them to solve problems.

A.REI.B.3 Solve linear equations and inequalities in one variable, including equations with coefficients represented by letters.

   Mathematical Practice Standards: 1, 2, 3, 4, 6, 7

TEACHING NOTES

Selected Response

1. *Error Analysis*: Students solve a proportion. If a student answers B or C the student either multiplied 9 by 4 incorrectly or divided 36 by 12 incorrectly. If the student answers D, the student does not understand proportion problems and is confusing cross products (x and 12 in opposite positions) with the mechanics required to solve a proportion.

2. *Error Analysis*: Students solve a word problem that requires proportional thinking. If the student answers A, he or she is setting up the proportion incorrectly. If a student answers B or C, he or she is either not setting up the proportion correctly or making mathematical errors, or both.

Constructed Response

3. Students use a scale to solve a problem. Ask students to name all of the units mentioned in the problem. Since the proportion will be scale = height of model to height of skyscraper, students need to recognize that the height of the model must be changed from feet to inches, because the scale is in inches.

Extended Response

4. Students solve a problem using percent discount. Have students write an equation to find the original price when they know the dollar amount of the discount and the purchase price. Then, have students write an equation to find the original price when they know the percent discount. For part (b), ask students which discount allowed the customer to purchase the higher priced item.

Common Core Standards Practice

Week 5

Selected Response

1. Solve for x.

$$\frac{x}{4} = \frac{9}{12}$$

  A 3

  B 4

  C 8

  D 12

2. A 15-ft tree casts an 18-ft shadow at the same time that a 24-ft tree casts a shadow. How long is the shadow of the 24-ft tree?

  A 20 ft

  B 21.6 ft

  C 27 ft

  D 28.8 ft

Constructed Response

3. An architect builds a scale model of a skyscraper for a land development proposal. The model is 2 ft tall. The scale of the model is 1 in. : 12.3 m.

How tall is the proposed skyscraper in meters? Show your work.

Extended Response

4. A department store advertises a sale where the customer chooses the discount. A customer may choose a flat discount of $15 off any purchase or 15% off the total purchase price. The final purchase price of an item was $150.

  a. What are the possible prices of the item before the discount the discount?

  b. Which discount represents a bigger savings in cost for the customer?

OVERVIEW

Looking Back	Mathematics of the Week	Looking Ahead
In Chapter 2, students used the Properties of Equality to solve equations, including equations that required them to use the Distributive Property to combine like terms (8.EE.C.7.a, 8.EE.C.7.b, A.REI.B.3).	Students write and solve inequalities using the Properties of Inequalities. They see how the process of solving equations and the process of solving inequalities is similar.	In Chapter 6, students will write two-variable inequalities so that they can graph the inequalities in the coordinate plane (A.CED.A.3, A.REI.D.12).

COMMON CORE CONTENT STANDARDS

A.CED.A.1 Create equations and inequalities in one variable and use them to solve problems.

A.REI.A.1 Explain each step in solving a simple equation as following from the equality of numbers asserted at the previous step, starting from the assumption that the original equation has a solution. Construct a viable argument to justify a solution method.

A.REI.B.3 Solve linear equations and inequalities in one variable, including equations with coefficients represented by letters.

Also **N.Q.A.2, A.CED.A.3**.

Mathematical Practice Standards: 1, 2, 3, 4, 7

TEACHING NOTES

Selected Response

1. *Error Analysis*: Students solve a one-variable inequality. If a student answers A, he or she divided by 3 rather than –3. If a student answers B, the student failed to reverse the inequality symbol when dividing by a negative. If the student answers D, the student added instead of dividing.

2. *Error Analysis*: Students match a one-variable inequality to a graph. If a student answers A or C, he or she does not understand the difference in meaning of an open circle and a closed circle. If a student answers B, the student does not associate ray to the right with greater than.

Constructed Response

3. Students solve an inequality in one variable and graph the result. Ask students what to do to with –3 to simplify the inequality. Ask students if dividing by a negative changes the inequality symbol, and ask students to justify their answer. For the graph, ask students if the graph requires open circles or closed circles.

Extended Response

4. Students use an inequality to solve a perimeter problem. Ask students to draw a rectangle and label all 4 sides. For the length, have students write an expression in terms of the width *w*. Ask students to write an expression that represents the perimeter. To write the correct inequality symbol, ask students which inequality symbol represents "can be no more than". For part (b), ask students what the upper restriction is for the length of a side (12), and then ask if there is a lower restriction.

Common Core Standards Practice

Week 6

Selected Response

1. Solve $-3x \geq -15$.

   A $x \geq -5$

   B $x \geq 5$

   C $x \leq 5$

   D $x \geq -12$

2. Which inequality is graphed below?

   A $b - 3 \geq 1$

   B $b + 3 < 1$

   C $b - 3 \leq 1$

   D $b + 3 > 1$

Constructed Response

3. Solve and graph the inequality $-3(g + 5) > 3$. Show your work and explain each step.

Extended Response

4. The length of a rectangle is 3 more than twice its width. If the perimeter of the rectangle can be no more than 78 ft, what are all of the possible widths of the rectangle?

   a. Write an inequality to solve the problem.

   b. Show your solution as a graph and describe the solution in words.

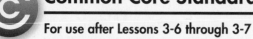

OVERVIEW

Looking Back	Mathematics of the Week	Looking Ahead
Earlier in Chapter 3, students wrote and solved inequalities using the Properties of Inequalities (A.CED.A.3, A.REI.B.3).	Students solve and graph absolute value in equalities. Students also graph compound inequalities and write compound inequalities for real-world situations.	In Chapter 5, students extend their understanding of absolute value to two-variable absolute value equations (F.BF.B.3). In Chapter 6, students graph two-variable inequalities (A.REI.D.12).

COMMON CORE CONTENT STANDARDS

A.SSE.A.1.b Interpret complicated expressions by viewing one or more of their parts as a single entity.

A.CED.A.1 Create equations and inequalities in one variable and use them to solve problems.

A.REI.B.3 Solve linear equations and inequalities in one variable, including equations with coefficients represented by letters.

Mathematical Practice Standards: 1, 2, 4, 7

TEACHING NOTES

Selected Response

1. *Error Analysis*: Students graph a compound inequality. If a student answers B or C, he or she is confusing the use of open and closed circles and which inequality symbols they represent. If a student answers B or D, he or she does not associate an arrow to the left with less than or an arrow to the right with greater than.

Constructed Response

2. Students solve an absolute value equation. Ask students to write two equations for the situation. Ask students why the expression $x + 8$ is equal to both 2 and –2. Ask students to substitute the solutions into the original equation to check their answers.

Extended Response

3. Students write and graph an inequality to solve a problem. Ask students to write an expression for what John plans to ask people other than his parents to contribute and then write an expression that includes the total that he expects to get in donations, including his parents. Ask students to write an inequality that shows the lower limit to the amount he expects to receive and an inequality that shows the upper limit to the amount he expects to receive. Ask students why these two inequalities can be combined into one compound inequality. Ask students whether "between $200 and $300" indicates the use of ≤ and ≥ symbols or < and > symbols. For part (b), confirm with students whether open or closed circles are appropriate for their graphs.

Common Core Standards Practice   Week 7

Selected Response

1. Graph the compound inequality $x > -3$ and $x \leq 5$.

A
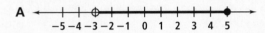

B
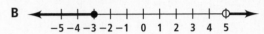

C

D

Constructed Response

2. Solve and graph $|x + 8| = 2$. Show your work.

Extended Response

3. John wants to raise between $200 and $300 for charity. His parents donated $50. John plans to ask others to contribute $10 each. How many people will need to contribute for John to reach his goal?

a. Write an inequality to solve the problem.

b. Show your solution as a graph and explain your solution in words.

OVERVIEW

Looking Back	Mathematics of the Week	Looking Ahead
In Chapter 1, students made tables and drew graphs for simple situations (7.EE.B.4.a, 8.EE.B.5, 8.EE.C.7.b). In Chapter 2, they solved equations using the Properties of Equality (A.REI.B.3).	Students make tables for real-world situations and draw graphs based on the tables. Students write two-variable equations for real-world situations	In Chapter 5, students will graph two-variable equations for linear functions (F.IF.C.7).

COMMON CORE CONTENT STANDARDS

A.CED.A.2 Create equations in two or more variables to represent relationships between quantities; graph equations on coordinate axes with labels and scales.

A.REI.D.10 Understand that the graph of an equation in two variables is the set of all its solutions plotted in the coordinate plane, often forming a curve...

F.IF.A.2 Use function notation, evaluate functions for inputs in their domains, and interpret statements that use function notation in terms of a context.

F.IF.B.4 For a function...interpret key features of graphs and tables in terms of the quantities, and sketch graphs showing key features given a verbal description of the relationship.

Mathematical Practice Standards: 1, 2, 4, 7

TEACHING NOTES

Selected Response

1. *Error Analysis*: Students write an equation from a table of paired data. If a student answers A or D, he or she has reversed the columns, using p for the first column and h for the second column. If the student answers D, the student correctly understand that the hours are multiplied by 3, resulting in the expression $3h$, but subtracts 10 rather than subtracting $3h$ from 10.

Constructed Response

2. Students make a table and a graph to show how variables in the equation are related. Ask students to find the value of h when $w = 1$, and continue with other values by 1s for w. Ask students to look at the values for h and find the difference between each pair of numbers. Ask students where they see this in the function rule. For the graph, suggest that students label the graph with a scale, so that all of the values they have found will fit. To find how tall the plant will be in 8 weeks, ask students if they would prefer to use the graph or extend the table.

Extended Response

3. Students write an equation to match a context, then they graph the equation to solve a problem. Ask students what the $4 represents. Ask what the variable m is multiplied by to find the cost of each mile. For part (b), ask students what the vertical intercept is and what that means in terms of the original problem. For part (c), ask students where they substitute the value $15 in the original equation and have them justify their answer.

Common Core Standards Practice **Week 8**

Selected Response

1. Which equation represents the data in the table?

Paint Cans Remaining per Hour

Number of Hours Worked, h	Number of Paint Cans Remaining, p
0	10
1	7
2	4
3	1

   A $p = 10h - 3$

   B $p = 3h - 10$

   C $p = 10 - 3h$

   D $p = 3 - 10h$

Constructed Response

2. The function rule $h = 3w + 2$ represents the height in centimeters h of a plant after w weeks of growth.

   a. Make a table of ordered pairs to show the height of the plant each week for 5 weeks.

   b. Graph the function. If the plant continues to grow at the same rate, how tall will it be after 8 weeks?

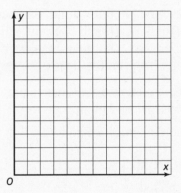

Extended Response

3. The posted rates for cab fare are $4 plus $1 per mile.

   a. Write an equation that represents total cab fare c for m miles.

   b. Sketch a graph of the equation on the axes provided.

   c. How many miles can a passenger travel in the cab for $15?

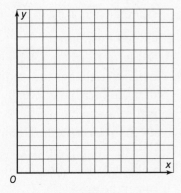

OVERVIEW

Looking Back	Mathematics of the Week	Looking Ahead
In Chapter 1, students made tables and created graphs for lines in the first quadrant (8.EE.B.5). In Chapter 4, students made tables for patterns and graphed the data in the tables in the first quadrant (F.IF.B.4, A.REI.D.10).	Students write function rules for real-world situations. They determine whether data in a table describes a function by using mapping diagrams and whether a graph shows a function using the vertical line test.	Students will apply their understanding of functions to linear functions in Chapter 5, exponential functions in Chapter 7, and quadratic functions in Chapter 9 (F.IF.B.4, F.IF.C.7).

COMMON CORE CONTENT STANDARDS

N.Q.A.2 Define appropriate quantities for the purpose of descriptive modeling.

A.CED.A.2 Create equations in two or more variables to represent relationships between quantities; graph equations on coordinate axes with labels and scales.

F.IF.A.1 Understand that a function from one set (called the domain) to another set (called the range) assigns to each element of the domain exactly one element of the range. If f is a function and x is an element of its domain, then $f(x)$ denotes the output of f corresponding to the input x. The graph of f is the graph of the equation $y = f(x)$.

F.IF.A.2 Use function notation, evaluate functions for inputs in their domains, and interpret statements that use function notation in terms of a context.

Mathematical Practice Standards: 1, 2, 4, 7

TEACHING NOTES

Selected Response

1. *Error Analysis*: Students evaluate the graphs of relations to determine which is not a function. If a student selects answer choices A, B, or C, he or she does not understand how to use the vertical-line test to determine whether a graph is a function or not.

Constructed Response

2. Students show understanding of vocabulary about relations and functions. For parts (a) and (b), ask students what is the domain and the range of the coordinates in the ordered pair (x, y) and then have them apply their answer to each ordered pair. For part (c), encourage students to make a mapping diagram, and then justify why the relation is not a function.

Extended Response

3. Students translate a sentence in words to an equation and use that equation to solve. The biggest challenge for students here is to remember that $3.00 represents the first game so that the variable g actually represents games greater than 1. So when $g = 1$, the value of c is for the second week. Having students verbalize this as they write the equation will help them in parts (b) and (c). In part (b), to find the cost of 4 games, students should recognize that they should use $g = 3$. In part (c), when they solve for the number of games and find $g = 7$, they should refer to the original situation to know that they need to add a game, to get the answer 8.

Common Core Standards Practice   **Week 9**

Selected Response

1. Which of the following is NOT a function?

   A 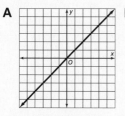   B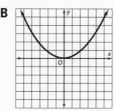

   C 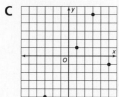   D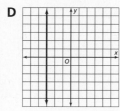

Constructed Response

2. Consider the relation {(7, 10), (7, 17), (7, 24), (7,31), (14, 10)}.

   a. What is the domain the of the relation?

   b. What is the range of the relation?

   c. Is the relation a function? Explain.

Extended Response

3. A bowling alley charges $3 for the first game and $1.50 for each additional game.

   a. Write a function rule that represents this situation.

   b. How much does it cost to bowl 4 games? Show your work.

   c. How many games can be played for a total cost of $13.50? Show your work.

OVERVIEW

Looking Back	Mathematics of the Week	Looking Ahead
In Chapter 4, students made tables and graphs for patterns (A.REI.D.10, F.IF.B.4). They also used function notation to describe patterns (F.IF.A.3).	Students write recursive and explicit formulas for arithmetic sequences using function notation.	In Algebra 2, students will extend their understanding of recursive and explicit formulas to geometric sequences and to finding sums of a finite series (F.BF.A.2, A.SSE.B.4).

COMMON CORE CONTENT STANDARDS

A.SSE.A.1.b Interpret complicated expressions by viewing one or more of their parts as a single entity.

F.IF.A.3 Recognize that sequences are functions, sometimes defined recursively, whose domain is a subset of the integers.

F.BF.A.1.a Determine an explicit expression, a recursive process, or steps for calculation from a context.

F.BF.A.2 Write arithmetic and geometric sequences both recursively and with an explicit formula, use them to model situations, and translate between the two forms.

Mathematical Practice Standards: 1, 2, 4, 6, 7, 8

TEACHING NOTES

Selected Response

1. *Error Analysis*: Students must choose a function that fits the terms of the sequence. If a student selects answer choice B, he or she does not understand that the common difference in this sequence must be added to the previous value, $f(n - 1)$. If a student selects answer choices C or D, he or she does not understand that to find $f(n)$, they must know the preceding number, which is $f(n - 1)$.

Constructed Response

2. Students will write a function for an arithmetic sequence and use that function to extend the sequence. Recommend to students that they write each term in the arithmetic sequence using the common denominator 8. This will help them more easily identify the common difference. For part (b), suggest to students that they check their answer by extending the sequence until there is a total of 12 terms.

Extended Response

3. Students show understanding of how to create and use explicit and recursive functions for sequences. For part (a), make sure students understand the difference between recursive and explicit and identify each function they write accordingly. For part (b), make sure that students use the correct number of $25 deposits. For part (c), look for reasonable explanations for using either the explicit or recursive function. Some students may prefer seeing amounts growing (or decreasing) by a constant amount and understanding what each step means, where others will prefer simplifying just one expression.

Common Core Standards Practice

Week 10

Selected Response

1. What is a recursive formula for the sequence 3, 24, 45, 66, 87, ... ?

   A $f(1) = 3; f(n) = f(n - 1) + 21$
   B $f(1) = 3; f(n) = f(n - 1) - 21$
   C $f(1) = 3; f(n) = f(n + 1) + 21$
   D $f(1) = 3; f(n) = f(n + 1) - 21$

Constructed Response

2. The sequence $\frac{1}{2}, \frac{7}{8}, 1\frac{1}{4}, 1\frac{5}{8}, 2$ is an arithmetic sequence.

   a. Write an explicit function for the sequence.

   b. Find the value of the 12th term of the sequence.

Extended Response

3. Stacy opens a savings account with a deposit of $100. She deposits an additional $25 every other week.

   a. Write an explicit function and a recursive function to represent this situation.

   b. Choose a function from part (a) and determine how much money will be in the account after 15 weeks if Stacy makes no additional deposits or withdrawals.

   c. Explain why you chose the function you used in part (b).

Common Core Standards Practice

Week 11

For use after Lessons 5-1 through 5-3

Algebra 1

OVERVIEW

Looking Back	Mathematics of the Week	Looking Ahead
In Chapter 4, students developed an understanding of function and function notation and made tables and graphs for linear and nonlinear rules (A.REI.D.10, F.IF.B.4).	Students find slope and write equations for direct variations and linear functions. They also graph linear equations using y-intercept and slope.	Later this chapter, students will use the point-slope and standard forms of linear functions to write and graph linear equations (F.LE.A.2, A.CED.A.2).

COMMON CORE CONTENT STANDARDS

N.Q.A.2 Define appropriate quantities for the purpose of descriptive modeling.

A.CED.A.2 Create equations in two or more variables to represent relationships between quantities; graph equations on coordinate axes with labels and scales.

F.IF.B.4 For a function that models a relationship between two quantities, interpret key features of graphs and tables in terms of the quantities, and sketch graphs showing key features given a verbal description of the relationship.

F.IF.B.6 Calculate and interpret the average rate of change of a function. . . .

F.IF.C.7.a Graph . . . linear and quadratic functions and show intercepts, maxima, and minima.

Mathematical Practice Standards: 1, 2, 4, 6, 7

TEACHING NOTES

Selected Response

1. *Error Analysis*: Students calculate the slope of a line given two points. If a student selects answer choice B, he or she has made a sign error when finding the slope. If a student selects answer choices A or D, he or she has found the difference between the y-coordinates and has not included dividing by the change in the x-coordinates.

2. *Error Analysis*: Students show understanding of direct variation by writing and using an equation. If a student selects answer choice A, he or she made a sign error in writing the direct variation equation. If a student selects answer choices C or D, he or she did not find k by dividing y by x (–6/2).

Constructed Response

3. Students show understanding of intercepts of a line, and how to make the scale for a line. Ask students where they will find an x-intercept (on the x-axis) and where they will find a y-intercept (on the y-axis.)

Extended Response

4. Students translate a word problem into an equation, which they graph and analyze. Ask students whether the 1,200 in the equation will be positive or negative and whether 15 in the equation will be positive or negative. Have them justify their reasoning. For part (b), if students are having trouble making the graph, you may wish to give parameters of 0 to 80 for the horizontal axis and 0 to 1,200 for the vertical axis. For part (c), remind students that the amount of gasoline must be 0 in the equation to indicate that it is all used.

Common Core Standards Practice   Week 11

Selected Response

1. Find the slope of the line that passes through the points $(-1, 6)$ and $(2, 15)$.

   A -9 **B** -3

   C 3 **D** 9

2. y varies directly with x. $y = -6$ when $x = 2$. Write a direct variation equation that relates y and x. Then find y when $x = 4$.

   A $y = 3x; y = 12$

   B $y = -3x; y = -12$

   C $y = 4x; y = 16$

   D $y = -4x; y = -16$

Constructed Response

3. Graph a line that has an x-intercept of 4 and a y-intercept of 3.

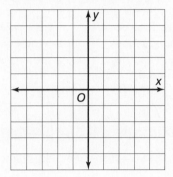

Extended Response

4. A research team uses a generator to power some crucial items at its base camp. The researchers begin the expedition with 1200 gallons of gasoline for the generator. They plan to use 15 gallons of gas per day.

   a. Write an equation in slope-intercept form that relates the amount of gasoline g remaining to the number of days d.

   b. Graph the equation from part (a).

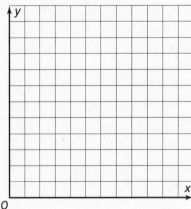

   c. The team expects to use all of the gasoline during their expedition. How many days do they expect the expedition to last? How do you know?

OVERVIEW

Looking Back	Mathematics of the Week	Looking Ahead
Earlier in chapter 5, students found slope and wrote equations for direct variations and linear functions. They also graphed linear equations using y-intercept and slope (A.CED.A.2, F.IF.B.4, F.IF.B.6, F.IF.C.7.a).	Students graph equations in point-slope form. Students use two points or information in a table, identifying two points, to write an equation in point-slope form.	Later this chapter, students will use equations in various forms to identify parallel and perpendicular lines (G.GPE.B.5). Also, students use the point-slope form to write equations for trend lines (S.ID.B.6.c)

COMMON CORE CONTENT STANDARDS

A.SSE.A.2 Use the structure of an expression to identify ways to rewrite it.

A.CED.A.2 Create equations in two or more variables to represent relationships between quantities; graph equations on coordinate axes with labels and scales.

F.IF.B.4 For a function that models a relationship between two quantities, interpret key features of graphs...and sketch graphs showing key features given a verbal description of the relationship.

F.IF.C.7.a Graph linear and quadratic functions and show intercepts, maxima, and minima.

F.BF.A.1.a Determine an explicit expression,...or steps for calculation from a context.

F.LE.A.2 Construct linear and exponential functions,...given a graph, a description of a relationship, or two input-output pairs (include reading these from a table).

Mathematical Practice Standards: 1, 4, 7

TEACHING NOTES

Selected Response

1. *Error Analysis*: Students write a linear equation in a given form. If a student selects answer choice B, he or she does not understand that for an x coordinate of -2, he or she must simplify $(x - (-2))$, which is $(x + 2)$, for $(x - x_1)$ in point-slope form. If a student selects answer choice C, he or she has substituted the x-coordinate for y_1 and the y-coordinate for x_1. If a student selects answer choice D, he or she is probably guessing and does not understand what to substitute for slope and the correct placement of the x and y coordinates in point-slope form.

Constructed Response

2. Students show understanding of parallel lines on a coordinate plane. For part (a), remind students to first determine what the slope of the line is and ask what that looks like to the left of $(0, -4)$ as well as to the right. For part (b), have students check their equation by substituting the coordinates of two points from their graph in the equation.

Extended Response

3. Students match equations to the graph of a line. Encourage students to determine the slope of the line, and eliminate any equation that does not have that slope. Then encourage students to identify the point that is indicated by each equation and determine if that point is on the line. Students may want to add a line for $x = 8$ and extend the line to find the value of y when $x = 8$.

Common Core Standards Practice

Week 12

Selected Response

1. Which is an equation of a line in point-slope form that has slope 7 and passes through $(-2, 6)$?

A $y - 6 = 7(x + 2)$

B $y - 6 = 7(x - 2)$

C $y + 2 = 7(x - 6)$

D $y - 6 = -2(x - 7)$

Constructed Response

2. a. Draw a line on the graph below that has the same slope as the line drawn and that passes through $(0, -4)$.

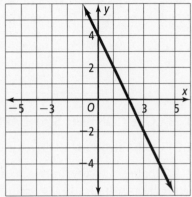

b. What is an equation of the line you drew?

Extended Response

3. Refer to the graph at the right. Write each equation in the correct column.

- $y - 4 = \frac{1}{2}(x - 8)$
- $y - 8 = \frac{1}{2}(x - 4)$
- $y - 1 = \frac{1}{2}(x + 10)$
- $y + 10 = 2(x - 1)$
- $y + 10 = \frac{1}{2}(x - 1)$

Possible Equation of the Line Drawn	NOT an Equation of the Line drawn

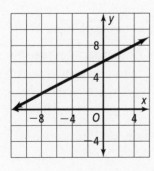

OVERVIEW

Looking Back	Mathematics of the Week	Looking Ahead
In Chapters 1 and 4, students graphed lines by making a table of points (A.REI.D.10). In Chapter 2, students solved literal equations (A.CED.A.4, A.REI.B.3).	Students graph lines using the *y*-intercept and slope. They write linear equations for real-world situations. Students rewrite linear equations in different forms. They also determine if the graphs of equations will be perpendicular or parallel by finding slope.	In Chapter 6, students will use their understanding of linear equations to graph and solve systems of linear equations (A.REI.C.6).

COMMON CORE CONTENT STANDARDS

A.SSE.A.2 Use the structure of an expression to identify ways to rewrite it.

A.CED.A.2 Create equations in two or more variables to represent relationships between quantities; graph equations on coordinate axes with labels and scales.

F.IF.B.4 For a function that models a relationship between two quantities, ... and sketch graphs showing key features given a verbal description of the relationship.

F.IF.C.7.a Graph linear and quadratic functions and show intercepts, maxima, and minima.

F.LE.A.2 Construct linear and exponential functions, ... given a graph, a description of a relationship, or two input-output pairs (include reading these from a table).

Mathematical Practice Standards: 1, 2, 4, 6, 7

TEACHING NOTES

Selected Response

1. *Error Analysis*: Students rewrite a linear equation in a different form. If a student selects answer choice A, he or she does not understand that an equation in standard form must be $Ax + By = C$. If a student selects answer choices B or D, he or she is probably guessing or has made two or more errors in their effort to transform from slope-intercept form to standard form.

Constructed Response

2. Students show understanding of parallel and perpendicular lines using equations. Ask students what they must know to determine if two lines are parallel or perpendicular. Ask students how they can get this information from the equations of the lines.

Extended Response

3. Students translate a word problem into an equation, which they graph and analyze. For part (a), ask students how many hours of tutoring are done by Jesse and by Lisa each in a month, assuming that there are four weeks in a month. This will help students account for all of the hours as they calculate the profit. For part (b), students may need help in determining the scale of the axes. Ask what value makes sense for the least and greatest values on the *y*-axis ($-\$200$ and more than $\$100$). For the *x*-axis, ask similar questions (0 to more than 20).

Common Core Standards Practice   Week 13

Selected Response

1. What is $y = -\dfrac{2}{3}x + 5$ written in standard form?

  A $3y = -2x + 5$

  B $3x - 2y = 15$

  C $2x + 3y = 15$

  D $2x - 3y = 5$

Constructed Response

2. Are the graphs of $2x + 5y = 10$ and $5x - 6y = 6$ *parallel*, *perpendicular*, or *neither*? Justify your answer.

Extended Response

3. Jesse and Lisa start a business tutoring students in math. They rent an office for $200 per month and charge $15 per hour per student.

  a. If they have 10 students each for one hour per week, how much profit do they make in a month? Write a linear equation to solve this problem.

  b. Graph the equation from part (a) and explain what it models.

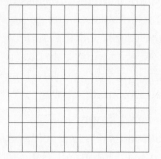

OVERVIEW

Looking Back	Mathematics of the Week	Looking Ahead
In earlier lessons in this chapter, students graphed equations based on the y-intercept or another point and the slope of the line as given in an equation (A.CED.A.2, A.CED.A.4, F.IF.B.4, F.IF.B.6).	Students graph scatter plots and trend lines, and find the equations of trend lines. They will translate the graph of $y = |x|$ by changing h and k in the equation $y = |x - h| + k$.	In Chapter 10, students will translate square root functions (F.IF.C.7.b). In Algebra 2, students will translate quadratic and exponential functions (F.IF.C.8).

COMMON CORE CONTENT STANDARDS

F.IF.C.7.b Graph square root, cube root, and piecewise-defined functions, including step functions and absolute value functions.

F.BF.B.3 Identify the effect on the graph of replacing $f(x)$ by $f(x) + k$, $k f(x)$, $f(kx)$, and $f(x + k)$ for specific values of k....

S.ID.B.6.a Fit a function to the data; use functions fitted to data to solve problems....

S.ID.B.6.c Fit a linear function for a scatter plot that suggests a linear association.

S.ID.C.7 Interpret the slope and the intercept of a linear model in the context of the data.

S.ID.C.8 Compute (using technology) and interpret the correlation coefficient of a linear fit.

S.ID.C.9 Distinguish between correlation and causation.

   Mathematical Practice Standards: 1, 2, 5, 6, 7
   Materials: Graphing calculator

TEACHING NOTES

Selected Response
1. *Error Analysis*: Students show understanding of how to translate a graph of an absolute value equation. If a student selects answer choices A, B, or C, he or she has some confusion about how h and k affect the graph of $y = |x - h| + k$.

Constructed Response
2. Students determine a scale for the data, and plot the data to show how the data relates. The greatest challenge for students in drawing a scatter plot is to determine the scale of the graph. Ask the students which data they plan to graph on the x-axis. From the data, ask students what scale they will use. Then have students determine a scale and appropriate interval for the y-axis. For part (b), discuss the idea of having an exact answer versus an approximate answer.

Extended Response
3. Students use technology to analyze a set of data points. For part (a), ask the students how to scale the graph. For part (b), students will need to use a graphing calculator or other technology. Ask students to indicate which data list should be the x-values and which the y-values. Remind students to check their entries before calculating the coefficient. For part (c), ask students to explain their understanding of the terms correlation and causation.

Common Core Standards Practice

Week 14

Selected Response

1. Which steps transform the graph of $y = |x|$ into the graph of $y = |x + 4| - 5$?

   A Translate 4 units right and 5 units up.
   B Translate 4 units left and 5 units up.
   C Translate 4 units right and 5 units down.
   D Translate 4 units left and 5 units down.

Constructed Response

2. **a.** Make a scatter plot and draw a trend line for the data at the right.

Student Test Scores

Hours Spent Studying	Test Score
3	70
6	88
2	68
7	90
1	60
4	73
8	92

   b. What would you expect a student who studied 5 hours to score on the test?

Extended Response

3. A teacher surveyed her students about the amount of physical activity they get each week. She then had their body mass index (BMI) measured.

   a. Use her data to make a scatter plot.

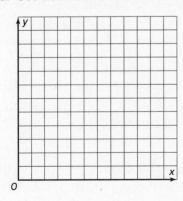

Body Mass Index

Active Hours	BMI
10	17
3	25
6	22
8	19
10	16
8	18
7	20

   b. Use a calculator to find the correlation coefficient.

   c. Is this relationship a correlation or causation or both? Explain how you know.

OVERVIEW

Looking Back	Mathematics of the Week	Looking Ahead
In Chapter 2, students solved one-variable equations using the properties of equality (A.REI.B.3). In Chapter 5, students graphed linear equations in two-variables (A.CED.A.2, F.IF.B.4, F.IF.C.7.a).	Students solve systems of equations using graphing, substitution, and elimination methods.	In Chapter 9, students will solve systems involving linear and quadratic functions (A.REI.C.7).

COMMON CORE CONTENT STANDARDS

A.REI.C.5 Prove that, given a system of two equations in two variables, replacing one equation by the sum of that equation and a multiple of the other produces a system with the same solutions.

A.REI.C.6 Solve systems of linear equations exactly and approximately (e.g., with graphs), focusing on pairs of linear equations in two variables.

A.REI.D.11 Explain why the x-coordinates of the points where the graphs of the equations $y = f(x)$ and $y = g(x)$ intersect are the solutions of the equation $f(x) = g(x)$; find the solutions approximately, e.g., using technology to graph the functions, make tables of values, or find successive approximations. Include cases where $f(x)$ and/or $g(x)$ are linear, polynomial, rational, absolute value, exponential, and logarithmic functions.

   Mathematical Practice Standards: 1, 2, 3, 4, 6, 7
   Materials: Graphing Calculator

TEACHING NOTES

Selected Response

1. *Error Analysis*: Students can use any method to solve this system of equations. If a student selects answer choice B, he or has the order of coordinates reversed. If a student selects answer choices C or D, they have made a sign error in finding the solution to the system.

Constructed Response

2. Students solve a system of linear equations using a given method. Ask students to identify which variable is easier to eliminate. Once students have found the value of x, remind them that they are not through until they have also found the value of y.

Extended Response

3. Students write a system of equations given a word problem and graph the equations to solve. For part (a), ask students to define what each variable represents. They will need to be consistent throughout the problem, referring back to their definitions as they solve and graph. For part (b), ask students to explain what the point of intersection means in terms of the situation. Students could rewrite their equations in slope-intercept form and graph on a graphing calculator or using other graphing programs.

Common Core Standards Practice   Week 15

Selected Response

1. What is the solution to the following system of equations?

   $3y - 2x = 11$
   $y + 2x = 9$

   A $(2, 5)$
   B $(5, 2)$
   C $(-2, -5)$
   D $(2, -5)$

Constructed Response

2. Solve the following system of equations by using elimination. Show your work.

   $x + 2y = 3$
   $4x - 2y = 7$

Extended Response

3. Antonio loves to go to the movies. He goes both at night and during the day. The cost of a matinee is $6. The cost of an evening show is $8. Antonio went to see a total of 5 movies and spent $36.

   a. How many of each type of movie did he attend? Write a system of equations and solve by graphing.

   b. Why is the intersection of the graphs of the linear equations the solution?

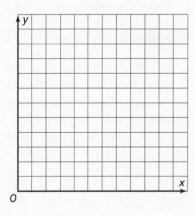

OVERVIEW

Looking Back	Mathematics of the Week	Looking Ahead
In Chapter 3, students graphed one-variable inequalities (7.EE.B.4.b). In Chapter 5, students graphed two-variable equations (A.CED.A.2, F.IF.B.4, F.IF.C.7.a).	Students determine if ordered pairs are solutions of two-variable inequalities and graph two-variable inequalities. Students solve systems of equations algebraically or by graphing.	Later in Chapter 6, students will graph systems of linear inequalities (A.REI.D.12). In Algebra 2, students will graph quadratic inequalities and solve systems of equations and inequalities (A.CED.A.3, A.REI.D.12)

COMMON CORE CONTENT STANDARDS

A.CED.A.3 Represent constraints by equations or inequalities, and by systems of equations and/or inequalities, and interpret solutions as viable or nonviable options in a modeling context.

A.REI.B.3 Solve linear equations and inequalities in one variable, including equations with coefficients represented by letters.

A.REI.C.6 Solve systems of linear equations exactly and approximately....

A.REI.D.12 Graph the solutions to a linear inequality in two variables as a half-plane, and graph the solution set to a system of linear inequalities in two variables as the intersection of the corresponding half-planes.

   Mathematical Practice Standards: 1, 4, 7, 8
   Materials: Graphing Calculator

TEACHING NOTES

Selected Response

1. *Error Analysis*: Students substitute coordinates into an inequality with two variables and evaluate the truth of the statement. If a student answers A, B, or C, he or she did not correctly substitute the given ordered pairs into the inequality, or did not correctly interpret the question to know that he or she are to find ordered pairs that are NOT solutions.

Constructed Response

2. Students will graph a half-plane to represent the solutions to a linear inequality. Ask students what they will do for the first step in graphing the equation. Ask students if the line of the graph should be solid or dashed. Finally, ask whether they should shade above or below the line, and how they know.

Extended Response

3. Students write a system of equations given a word problem and graph the equations to solve. For part (a), ask students to define x and y, and then write equations for total shots and for total points. For part (b), ask students to determine the scale for each axis. They should recognize that $(0, 35)$ and $(35, 0)$ should be included. Students could rewrite their equations in slope-intercept form and graph the equations on a graphing calculator.

Common Core Standards Practice

Week 16

Selected Response

1. Which ordered pair is NOT a solution of $y > 3x + 4$?

A $(2, 12)$
B $(0, 5)$
C $(-2, 1)$
D $(1, 7)$

Constructed Response

2. Graph $3x + 2y > 6$.

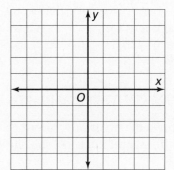

Extended Response

3. The Movers scored a total of 80 points in their game last night against the Shakers. The Movers made no one-point shots, and a total of 35 two-point and three-point shots.

  a. How many two-point shots did the Movers make? How many three-point shots did the Movers make? Write and solve a system of equations that can be used to solve this problem.

  b. Graph the system of equations.

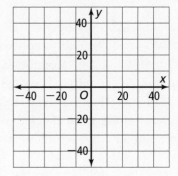

OVERVIEW

Looking Back	Mathematics of the Week	Looking Ahead
In Chapter 3, students graphed one-variable inequalities (7.EE.B.4.b). In earlier lessons in this chapter, students graphed systems of equations as well as two-variable inequalities (A.REI.C.6, A.REI.D.12).	Students graph systems of inequalities and determine the region of overlap that satisfies the two inequalities. Students write inequalities for a real-world situation and solve those systems of inequalities.	In Algebra 2, students will deepen their understanding of systems of inequalities and will apply this understanding to linear programming to find feasible solutions for real-world problems (A.REI.D.12).

COMMON CORE CONTENT STANDARDS

A.CED.A.3 Represent constraints by equations or inequalities, and by systems of equations and/or inequalities, and interpret solutions as viable or nonviable options in a modeling context.

A.REI.D.12 Graph the solutions to a linear inequality in two variables as a half-plane (excluding the boundary in the case of a strict inequality), and graph the solution set to a system of linear inequalities in two variables as the intersection of the corresponding half-planes.

Mathematical Practice Standards: 1, 2, 3, 4, 6, 7

TEACHING NOTES

Selected Response

1. *Error Analysis*: Students match graph to two inequalities that form a system of inequalities. If a student selects answer choices B or D, he or she is not correctly graphing $y > -x + 3$, which should have a negative slope. If a student selects answer choice C, the students is not shading $y < x + 2$ correctly.

Constructed Response

2. Students show understanding of possible combinations of systems of linear inequalities. Ask students when a system of equations will have no solution. Ask students how they can apply their answer to a system of inequalities. Ask them what must be true of the shading.

Extended Response

3. Students write a system of inequalities given a word problem and graph the inequalities to solve. For part (a) ask students to define x and y. Then ask, what inequality represents "she will sell more than 50 bracelets." For part (b), ask students what the inequality for the 50 bracelets will look like when they graph it. For both inequalities in part (a), ask students whether the lines will be dashed or solid. Ask students to indicate what they will use for the scale on each axis, and justify their choice. For part (c), ask students to check their answer in the context of the original situation using the system that they wrote in part (a).

Common Core Standards Practice

Week 17

Selected Response

1. Which is the graph of the solution for the system of inequalities?

$$y > -x + 3$$
$$y < x + 2$$

A 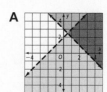 **B**

C 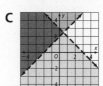 **D**

Selected Response

2. Sketch the graph of a system of inequalities that has no solution. Describe how you know that the system has no solution.

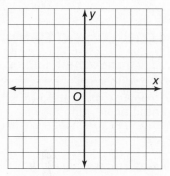

Extended Response

3. Sarah is selling bracelets and necklaces to make money for her summer vacation. The bracelets cost $2 and the necklaces cost $3. She needs to make at least $500. Sarah knows that she will sell more than 50 bracelets.

   a. Write a system of inequalities for Sarah's situation.

   b. Graph the system of inequalities.

   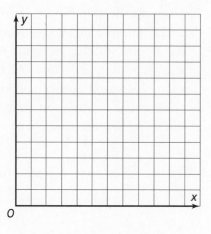

   c. How many bracelets and necklaces could Sarah sell? Explain how you know that your solution is reasonable.

OVERVIEW

Looking Back	Mathematics of the Week	Looking Ahead
In Grade 8, students used the properties of exponents to simplify expressions with integer values of exponents (8.EE.A.1).	Students use the properties of exponents to simplify expressions containing rational exponents.	Later in Chapter 7, students will write, solve, and graph equations that include rational exponents (A.CED.A.2, F.IF.C.7.e).

COMMON CORE CONTENT STANDARDS

N.RN.A.1 Explain how the definition of the meaning of rational exponents follows from extending the properties of integer exponents to those values, allowing for a notation for radicals in terms of rational exponents.

N.RN.A.2 Rewrite expressions involving radicals and rational exponents using the properties of exponents.

   Mathematical Practice Standards: 1, 3, 6, 7

TEACHING NOTES

Selected Response

1. *Error Analysis*: Students simplify an expression using properties of exponents. If a student selects answer choices A or B, he or she does not understand the meaning of a negative power. If a student selects answer choice D, the student did not square 8; he or she multiplied 2 times 8 instead.

Constructed Response

2. Students use properties of exponents and multiplication to simplify. Ask students how the Commutative Property of Multiplication can help them rearrange coefficients and variables to help simplify the expression. Ask students to explain how they will find the exponent for a and the exponent for t, justifying their answers using the properties of exponents.

Extended Response

3. Students show understanding of exponent rules. Ask students to substitute a value for x and another value for y, making sure $y > x$. Then have students use another set of values. Ask if they think the equation may be true for all sets of values where $y > x$. Do caution students that just because the two expressions are equivalent for certain values—or even many values—it does not prove they are equivalent for all values. Challenge students to show that the two expressions are equivalent by rewriting each side of the equation without using denominators to see if they can find an expression to which both are equivalent.

Common Core Standards Practice

Week 18

Selected Response

1. What is the simplified form of $8^{-2}a^4 b^{-3}$?

   A $-16a^4 3b$

   B $-64a^4 b$

   C $\dfrac{a^4}{64b^3}$

   D $\dfrac{a^4}{16b^3}$

Constructed Response

2. Simplify the expression

   $\left(3a^{\frac{1}{5}} \cdot 4t^{\frac{2}{7}}\right)\left(2a^{\frac{4}{5}} \cdot t^{\frac{4}{7}}\right)$. Show your work.

Extended Response

3. Your classmate writes that if $y > x$, then $\dfrac{a^x}{a^y} = \dfrac{1}{a^{(y-x)}}$ for all real numbers x and y.

   Is your classmate correct? Explain how you know and show examples to justify your explanation.

OVERVIEW

Looking Back	Mathematics of the Week	Looking Ahead
In Chapter 4, students graphed non-linear functions using tables. In earlier lessons in this chapter, students used the properties of exponents to simplify expressions (A.REI.D.10, F.IF.B.4).	Students simplify radical expressions by first rewriting the expressions using rational exponents. Students graph exponential functions by making tables for the function rules and graphing points.	In Algebra 2, students will graph exponential functions and their inverses, as well as logarithmic functions (F.IF.C.7.e).

COMMON CORE CONTENT STANDARDS

N.RN.A.2 Rewrite expressions involving radicals...using the properties of exponents.

A.CED.A.2 Create equations in two or more variables to represent relationships between quantities; graph equations on coordinate axes with labels and scales.

F.IF.B.5 Relate the domain of a function...to the quantitative relationship it describes.

F.LE.A.2 Construct...exponential functions,...given a graph, [or] a description of a relationship....

F.LE.B.5 Interpret the parameters in a linear or exponential function in terms of a context.

Mathematical Practice Standards: 1, 2, 4, 6, 7
Materials: Graphing calculator

TEACHING NOTES

Selected Response

1. *Error Analysis*: Students simplify radical expressions using properties of exponents. If a student selects answer choice A, he or she does not multiply the two 8s properly. If a student selects answer choice B, he or she ignores the variable a in the first radical. If a student selects answer choice D, he or she did not take the cube root of the expression.

Constructed Response

2. Students show understanding of the defined variables in an exponential growth problem. To help students understand what $x = -5$ means with respect to the value of y, ask students what the value of y represents when $x = 0$ and what the value of y means when $x = 1$.

Extended Response

3. Students write, graph, and evaluate an exponential equation for an exponential growth problem. For part (a), remind students that their function should grow from a population of 8 at month 0. Encourage students to make a table that shows the growth in mouse population for several months. Then ask them to compare their table with the results they get from the equation when they evaluate for several months. For part (b), ask students what value they should substitute for x, and why (24, because x represents months and there are 24 months in two years). For part (c), ask students how many months they think should be represented on the x-axis and what number of mice should be included on the scale on the y-axis. Students could graph the equation using a graphing calculator.

Common Core Standards Practice   Week 19

Selected Response

1. Write the expression $\sqrt[3]{8a^2} \cdot \sqrt[3]{8ab^5}$ in exponential form.

A $8^{\frac{1}{3}}ab^2$

B $8^{\frac{2}{3}}a^{\frac{1}{3}}b^{\frac{5}{3}}$

C $4ab^{\frac{5}{3}}$

D $64a^3b^5$

Constructed Response

2. A population of prairie dogs doubles every year in the plains of North Dakota. The number of prairie dogs can be modeled by the equation $y = 400 \cdot 2^x$, where x is the number of years after a scientist measures the population size. When $x = -5$, what does the value of y represent?

Extended Response

3. There are 8 mice in an attic. Their population is growing at a rate of 15% per month.

a. Write an exponential growth equation to model this situation.

b. How many mice will there be in the attic in two years if nothing is done to slow down or stop the growth?

c. Sketch a graph of the function.

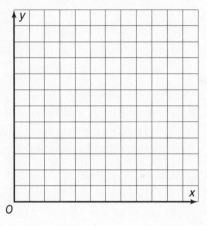

OVERVIEW

Looking Back	Mathematics of the Week	Looking Ahead
In Chapter 4, students graphed non-linear functions using tables, and wrote recursive and explicit rules for arithmetic sequences (A.CED.A.2, F.IF.B.4, F.IF.C.7.b).	Students use exponential functions to describe growth and decay. Students use recursive and explicit functions for geometric sequences.	In Algebra 2, students will graph exponential and logarithmic functions (F.IF.C.7.e).

COMMON CORE CONTENT STANDARDS

A.SSE.A.1.a Interpret parts of an expression, such as terms, factors, and coefficients.

F.IF.A.3 Recognize that sequences are functions, sometimes defined recursively, whose domain is a subset of the integers.

F.BF.A.1.a Determine an explicit expression, a recursive process....

F.LE.A.1.c Recognize situations in which a quantity grows or decays by a constant percent rate per unit interval relative to another.

F.LE.A.2 Construct linear and exponential functions,... given a graph, a description of a relationship, or two input-output pairs (include reading these from a table).

Mathematical Practice Standards: 1, 2, 3, 4, 6, 7, 8
Materials: Graphing calculator

TEACHING NOTES

Selected Response

1. *Error Analysis*: Students choose a pair of equations for a geometric sequence. If a student selects answer choice A or D, he or she does not realize that a_1 should be the first number in the sequence. If a student selects answer choice C or D, he or she is confusing arithmetic and geometric sequences.

Constructed Response

2. Students write formulas to show understanding of a geometric sequence provided in context. Ask students what a_1 and r must be for the recursive formula. Ask them why both values are 2. Ask students how this information also helps them write the explicit formula.

Extended Response

3. Students write and analyze a function to represent an exponential decay problem. For part (a) ask students what *depreciates* means and then ask whether this situation is an example of growth or decay. For part (b), ask what the original value (base) is. If students indicate the base is 0.15, rather than (1 − 0.15), have them make a table for the situation. This will help them see that the decrease is 15% of the original value, but the resulting value is 85% of the original value. For part (c), remind students to use the Order of Operations as they simplify.

Common Core Standards Practice

Selected Response

1. Which is a recursive definition for the following geometric sequence?
3, 9, 27, 81,...

A $a_1 = 0; a_n = 3(a_{n-1})$
B $a_1 = 3; a_n = 3(a_{n-1})$
C $a_1 = 3; a_n = 3 + a_{n-1}$
D $a_1 = 0; a_n = 3 + a_{n-1}$

Constructed Response

2. Brian has 2 parents, 4 grandparents, 8 great-grandparents, and so on.

a. Write an explicit formula and recursive formula for the number of ancestors Brian has in a generation if he goes back to the nth generation.

b. Interpret the parts of the formula and explain their meaning within the context of this situation.

Extended Response

3. Suppose that a new house is worth $200,000 and that it depreciates at a rate of 15% a year.

a. Explain this situation in terms of growth or decay.

b. Construct a function to model this situation.

c. Estimate the value of the house after 5 years.

OVERVIEW

Looking Back	Mathematics of the Week	Looking Ahead
In Chapter 1, students evaluated expressions, including expressions with exponents. Students also used the Order of Operations and the Distributive Property (A.SSE.A.1).	Students name polynomials by degree and number of terms. They add, subtract, and multiply binomials, including the special cases squaring a binomial and finding the product of a sum or difference.	In the following lessons of this chapter, students will factor polynomials (A.SSE.A.1.a).

COMMON CORE MATHEMATICAL CONTENT STANDARDS

A.APR.A.1 Understand that polynomials form a system analogous to the integers, namely, they are closed under the operations of addition, subtraction, and multiplication; add, subtract, and multiply polynomials.

Common Core Mathematical Practice Standards: 1, 6, 7 8

TEACHING NOTES

Selected Response

1. *Error Analysis*: Students square a binomial. If a student selects answer choice A, the student multiplied $(x + 4)$ by 2, rather than squaring the quantity. If a student selects answer choice C, he or she squared the first and last terms, but did not square the expression. If a student selects answer choice D, he or she may be confused about the rule for squaring a binomial.

Constructed Response

2. Students add and subtract polynomials to simplify and compare to another polynomial. Ask students how the negative sign before an expression affects every term in the expression, to confirm that the students have a firm grasp on multiplying by a negative.

Extended Response

3. Students multiply two binomials and demonstrate an understanding of the vocabulary of polynomials. For part (a), have students who are having difficulty correctly finding the middle term draw an area model to show each part that makes up the product. For part (b), ask students to state their understanding of degree of a polynomial and number of terms in a polynomial.

Common Core Standards Practice

Week 21

Selected Response

1. Which expression is equivalent to $(x + 4)^2$?

- **A** $2x + 8$
- **B** $x^2 + 8x + 16$
- **C** $x^2 + 16$
- **D** $x^2 + 16x + 8$

Constructed Response

2. Classify each expression as equivalent to $2x^2 + 17x$ or **NOT** equivalent to $2x^2 + 17x$. Write each expression inside the appropriate box below.

$(4x^2 + 10x + 7) - (2x^2 - 7x + 7)$

$x(2x + 17)$

$5x^2 - (3x^2 + 12x) + 5x$

$(2x^2 + 5x^2) + (-5x^2 + x + x + 15x)$

Expressions Equivalent to $2x^2 + 17x$	Expressions Not Equivalent to $2x^2 + 17x$

Extended Response

3. The length of a rectangular sandbox is $3x + 5$. The width of the sandbox is $x - 3$.

a. What polynomial in standard form represents the area of the sandbox?

b. Name the polynomial based on its degree and number of terms.

OVERVIEW

Looking Back	Mathematics of the Week	Looking Ahead
In Grade 7, students used the formula for the area of a circle (7.G.B.4). In Chapter 1, students evaluated expressions, including expressions with exponents. Also, students used the Order of Operations and the Distributive Property (A.SSE.A.1).	Students name polynomials by degree and number of terms. They add, subtract, and multiply binomials, including the special cases of squaring a binomial and finding the product of a sum or difference.	In the following lessons of this chapter, students will factor polynomials (A.SSE.A.1.a). In Chapter 11, students will multiply binomials to add and subtract rational expressions (A.APR.D.6).

COMMON CORE MATHEMATICAL CONTENT STANDARDS

A.APR.A.1 Understand that polynomials form a system analogous to the integers,…add, subtract, and multiply polynomials.

> **Common Core Mathematical Practice Standards:** 1, 2, 6, 7, 8
> **Materials:** Calculator

TEACHING NOTES

Selected Response

1. *Error Analysis*: Students demonstrate an understanding degree of a polynomial. If a student selects answer choice A, he or she may think that the degree of a monomial is the degree of the variable with the greatest exponent, rather than the sum of the exponents of the term's variables. If a student selects answer choices C or D, he or she may have guessed and does not understand degrees of a monomial.

Constructed Response

2. Students cube a binomial and demonstrate an understanding of the vocabulary of polynomials. For part (a), have students who are having difficulty draw an area model for $(x + 2)(x + 2)$ and then draw an area model for $(x^2 + 4x + 4)(x + 2)$. For part (b), ask students to state their understanding of the degree of a polynomial.

Extended Response

3. Students apply their understanding of the products of a polynomial to a situation in which they subtract products to find the area of a shaded region. For part (a), if a student does not recognize the region meant by "rectangle," have them color the bottom half of the circle. For part (b), have students write the formula for the area of a circle and substitute for r. For part (c), ask students if all of the area of the circle is needed to find the answer. For part (d), encourage students to be careful as they substitute the value of the radius.

Common Core Standards Practice   Week 22

Selected Response

1. What is the degree of the monomial $3x^4yz$?

   A 4

   B 6

   C 7

   D 8

Constructed Response

2. **a.** Simplify the expression $(x + 2)^3$.

   b. Name the polynomial based on its degree.

Extended Response

3. Refer to the figure shown. When necessary, use 3.14 for π.

   a. What is an expression for the area of the rectangle? Simplify your answer.

   b. What is an expression for the area of the circle? Simplify your answer.

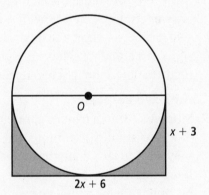

$x + 3$

$2x + 6$

   c. What is an expression for the area of the shaded region? Simplify your answer.

   d. If the radius of the circle is 5 cm, what is the area of the shaded region?

OVERVIEW

Looking Back	Mathematics of the Week	Looking Ahead
In Chapter 1, students used the Distributive Property to combine like terms. In the earlier lessons in this chapter, students multiplied polynomials (A.APR.A.1) and factored binomials (A.SSE.A.1.a).	Students factor special cases: perfect square trinomials and the difference of two squares. Students factor polynomials with 4 terms using grouping techniques.	In Chapter 9, students will solve quadratic equations using factoring (A.REI.B.4). Students will also solve equations by completing the square and will derive and use the quadratic formula (A.REI.B.4.a).

COMMON CORE MATHEMATICAL CONTENT STANDARDS

A.SSE.A.1.a Interpret parts of an expression, such as terms, factors, and coefficients.

A.SSE.A.1.b Interpret complicated expressions by viewing one or more of their parts as a single entity.

A.SSE.A.2 Use the structure of an expression to identify ways to rewrite it.

Common Core Mathematical Practice Standards: 1, 2, 4, 7

TEACHING NOTES

Selected Response

1. *Error Analysis*: Students factor a polynomial with 4 terms by grouping. If a student selects answer choice A, he or she may have incorrectly factored the first two terms. If a student selects answer choice B, he or she could have made one or more errors with respect to signs. If a student selects answer choice D, the student likely made a sign error and incorrectly factored the first two terms.

Constructed Response

2. Students factor a trinomial into the square of a binomial to describe a real-world context. Students should determine that the trinomial is the square of a binomial. Some students may wish to factor the trinomial by 4 first, which will result in an answer of $2(3x + 4)$. Remind these students that they must account for the 4 by multiplying it back into the binomial, giving a final answer of $(6x + 8)$.

Extended Response

3. Students multiply, subtract, and factor polynomials in an area problem. Students are will define each part of a polynomial in the context of the situation. For part (a), students' diagrams should show that x, the width of the pathway, is on each side of the garden's side lengths. For part (b), ask students to write a word description for the information supplied in the problem, as in "Area of sidewalk only = area of sidewalk and garden − area of garden." This will help students recognize that 24, the area of the garden and the area of the sidewalk only, is used twice in the equation to find the width of a side of the pathway.

Common Core Standards Practice

Week 23

Selected Response

1. Factor the following polynomial.

$$7x^4 - 4x^3 + 28x^2 - 16x$$

A $x(7x^2 - 4)(x + 4)$

B $x(7x + 4)(x^2 - 4)$

C $x(7x - 4)(x^2 + 4)$

D $x(7x^2 + 4)(x - 4)$

Constructed Response

2. The area of a square window is $36x^2 + 96x + 64$. What is a side length of the window?

Extended Response

3. A rectangular garden measuring 4 m by 6 m is to have a pathway x meters wide installed around its perimeter. The area of the pathway will be equal to the area of the garden.

a. Make a sketch of this situation and define each part of the polynomial.

b. What will be the width of the pathway?

OVERVIEW

Looking Back	Mathematics of the Week	Looking Ahead
In Chapter 4, students graphed non-linear functions (A.REI.D.10). In Chapter 8, students multiplied and factored polynomials (A.APR.A.1).	Students find the axis of symmetry of a parabola and graph quadratic functions. Students solve quadratic equations. Students use quadratic functions to model real-world situations.	In Algebra 2, students will solve quadratic equations with complex solutions (N.CN.A.1). Students will use factoring techniques to identify zeros of rational functions (A.APR.B.3).

COMMON CORE MATHEMATICAL CONTENT STANDARDS

F.IF.B.4 For a function . . . interpret key features of graphs and tables . . . , and sketch graphs showing key features given a verbal description of the relationship.

F.IF.B.5 Relate the domain of a function to its graph . . .

F.IF.C.7.a Graph . . . quadratic functions and show intercepts, maxima, and minima.

F.IF.C.8.a Use the process of factoring . . . in a quadratic function to show zeros, extreme values, and symmetry of the graph, and interpret these in terms of a context.

Common Core Mathematical Practice Standards: 1, 2, 4, 6, 7
Materials: Graphing calculator

TEACHING NOTES

Selected Response

1. *Error Analysis*: Students find the vertex of a parabola. If a student selects answer choice A or B, he or she may be using the 1 and 3 in the given equation to write an ordered pair. If a student selects answer choice C, he or she may have confused values of x and y that they found and incorrectly wrote the ordered pair for the vertex.

Constructed Response

2. Students graph a quadratic function and use the graph to find its zeros. For part (a), some students will make a table to find and then graph points. Encourage these students to find the vertex and use the vertex and the axis of symmetry to mirror points as they make the graph. For part (b), ask students how they can use the graph of the function to find the solutions of the equation. Have students articulate that the solutions of the equation are where $y = 0$ on the graph of the function.

Extended Response

3. Students solve a real-world problem using a quadratic function. For part (a), ask students what to substitute for to write an equation that answers the question. Have students justify their answers. For the graph, have students check their graph with a graphing calculator. For part (b), have students identify the real-world context for the y-intercept, vertex, and x-intercept.

Common Core Standards Practice

Selected Response

1. What is the vertex of the parabola with equation $y = 3x^2 + 1$?

   A $(1, 3)$

   B $(3, 1)$

   C $(1, 0)$

   D $(0, 1)$

Constructed Response

2. **a.** Graph the equation $y = 4x^2 - 4$.

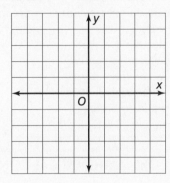

   b. Find the solutions to $4x^2 - 4 = 0$.

Extended Response

3. You throw a ball into the air from a building. The ball's height h, in feet, after t seconds can be modeled by the function $h(t) = -16t^2 + 32t + 48$.

   a. After how many seconds will the ball hit the ground? Solve by factoring and by sketching a graph.

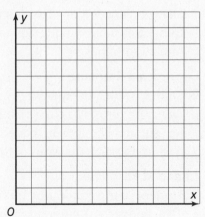

   b. Interpret the key features of the graph and how they relate to this situation.

OVERVIEW

Looking Back	Mathematics of the Week	Looking Ahead
In Chapter 5, students multiplied and factored polynomials (A.APR.A.1). Earlier in Chapter 9, students graphed quadratic functions using the vertex, the line of symmetry, and solved quadratic equations by graphing and by finding square roots (A.REI.B.4.b).	Students solve equations by graphing, factoring, and completing the square.	In Lesson 9-6, students use completing the square to drive the quadratic formula (A.REI.B.4.a). In Algebra 2, students use completing the square to find the center and radius of a circle from its equation (G.GPE.A.1).

COMMON CORE MATHEMATICAL CONTENT STANDARDS

A.SSE.A.2 Use the structure of an expression to identify ways to rewrite it.

A.SSE.B.3.a Factor a quadratic expression to reveal the zeros of the function it defines.

A.APR.B.3 Identify zeros of polynomials when suitable factorizations are available, and use the zeros to construct a rough graph of the function defined by the polynomial.

A.REI.A.2 Solve simple rational and radical equations in one variable....

A.REI.B.4 Solve quadratic equations in one variable.

A.REI.B.4.a Use the method of completing the square to transform any quadratic equation in x into an equation of the form $(x - p)^2 = q$ that has the same solutions....

Common Core Mathematical Practice Standards: 1, 2, 4, 6, 7

TEACHING NOTES

Selected Response

1. *Error Analysis*: Students solve a quadratic equation by factoring. If a student selects answer choices A or C, he or she may have added $2x$ to each side rather than subtracting from each side, or made sign errors. If a student selects only B or only D, he or she did not find all solutions.

Constructed Response

2. Students solve an equation by completing the square and graphing the related function using the zeros. For part (a), ask students what must be added to $x^2 + 4x$ to make it a perfect square. For part (b), have students to find the approximate values of their answers in part (a) to graph the zeros of the function.

Extended Response

3. Students use a quadratic expression to solve a real-world problem about a rectangular area. For part (a), students factor a trinomial as the square of a binomial. For part (b), ask students, based on their answer to part (a), what type of quadrilateral the rooftop must be. For part (c), ask students what equation they will use to find the value of x.

Common Core Standards Practice

Week 25

Selected Response

1. Choose all the solutions of $x^2 - 8 = 2x$.

   A $x = -4$

   B $x = -2$

   C $x = 2$

   D $x = 4$

Constructed Response

2. a. Solve $x^2 + 4x = -1$ by completing the square.

b. Use the zeros you found in part (a) to graph the function defined by the polynomial equation $x^2 + 4x = y - 1$.

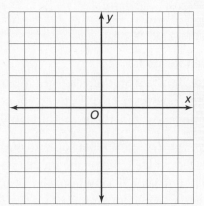

Extended Response

3. The area of a rooftop can be expressed as $4x^2 + 4x + 1$. The rooftop is a quadrilateral.

   a. What expression describes the length of one side of the rooftop?

   b. What type of quadrilateral is the rooftop? How do you know?

   c. If the area of the rooftop is 441 m^2, what is x?

OVERVIEW

Looking Back	Mathematics of the Week	Looking Ahead
In Chapter 8, students factored expressions (A.SSE.A.1.a). In Lesson 9-4, students used factoring to solve quadratic equations (A.REI.B.4.b).	Students use completing the square and the quadratic formula to solve equations.	In Algebra 2, students will use the quadratic formula to solve equations with complex solutions (N.CN.C.7).

COMMON CORE MATHEMATICAL CONTENT STANDARDS

A.CED.A.1 Create equations…in one variable and use them to solve problems.

A.REI.B.4.b Solve quadratic equations by…the quadratic formula and factoring,….

F.IF.C.8.a Use the process of factoring and completing the square in a quadratic function to show zeros.…

Also **A.SSE.B.3.b, A.REI.A.1, A.REI.B.4.a**.

Common Core Mathematical Practice Standards: 1, 2, 4, 6, 7
Materials: Calculator

TEACHING NOTES

Selected Response

1. *Error Analysis*: Students solve a quadratic equation by completing a square. If a student selects answer B, C, or D, the student did not correctly evaluate the radical expression or did not substitute the expression in the equation and simplify correctly.

2. *Error Analysis:* Students solve an equation using the quadratic formula. If a student selects answer choice B, he or she may have used b rather than $-b$ in the quadratic formula, causing a sign error. If a student selects answer choice C, he or she probably did not divide by $2a$ when using the quadratic formula. If a student selects answer choice D, he or she may have made more than one calculation error.

Constructed Response

3. Students solve a quadratic equation for a real-world situation. For part (a), ask students what the height of the bird is when it is skimming the water. For part (b), ask students to confirm their answers by graphing the function and finding its zeros.

Extended Response

4. Students use a quadratic function to solve a real-world problem about volume. For part (a), remind students that there are three factors that contribute to the volume. For part (b), ask students how to use the volume 6 ft³ to write an equation. For part (c), ask students how they will use the values they found for x to find possible lengths of sides and how they will know if there is an extraneous solution for this situation.

Common Core Standards Practice   Week 26

Selected Response

1. Solve $x^2 + 20x = -40$ by completing the square.

   A $x = -10 \pm \sqrt{60}$

   B $x = 10 \pm \sqrt{60}$

   C $x = -10 \pm \sqrt{140}$

   D $x = 10 \pm \sqrt{140}$

2. Solve $x^2 + 4x - 2 = 3$ by using the quadratic formula.

   A $x = 1, -5$

   B $x = -1, 5$

   C $x = 2, -10$

   D $x = 4, -8$

Constructed Response

3. The flight path of a bird is modeled by the function $y = x^2 - 14x + 16$, where y is the eagle's height in centimeters above the water and x is time in seconds.

   a. Find the roots of the equation by completing the square. Show your work. Write your answer as a decimal.

   b. What does this solution tell you about the bird's flight?

Extended Response

4. You can use the formula $V = lwh$ to find the volume of a box.

   a. Write a quadratic equation in standard form that represents the volume of the box.

   b. The volume of the box is 6 ft^3. Solve the quadratic equation for x.

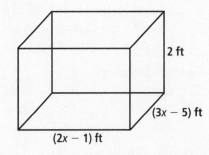

2 ft

$(3x - 5)$ ft

$(2x - 1)$ ft

   c. Use the solution from part (b) to find the length and width of the box. Describe any extraneous solutions.

OVERVIEW

Looking Back	Mathematics of the Week	Looking Ahead
In Chapter 7, students applied the properties of exponents to radical expressions (N.RN.A.2). In Chapter 8, students squared binomials (A.APR.A.1). In Chapter 9, students solved quadratic equations (A.REI.B.4.b).	Students use the Pythagorean Theorem and its converse. Students simplify, add, subtract, and multiply radical expressions. Finally, students solve radical equations and identify extraneous solutions.	In Algebra 2, students will work with imaginary numbers (N.CN.A.1), find the inverse of functions (F.BF.B.4.a), and graph radical functions (F.IF.C.7.b).

COMMON CORE MATHEMATICAL CONTENT STANDARDS

A.CED.A.4 Rearrange formulas to highlight a quantity of interest, using the same reasoning as in solving equations.

A.REI.A.2 Solve simple rational and radical equations in one variable, and give examples showing how extraneous solutions may arise.

Common Core Mathematical Practice Standards: 1, 2, 4, 7

TEACHING NOTES

Selected Response

1. Students use the Pythagorean Theorem to find the hypotenuse of a triangle. If a student selects answer choice A, he or she may incorrectly interpret the Pythagorean Theorem. If a student selects answer choice B, he or she may incorrectly simplified the square root of 26. If a student selects answer choice C, the student may have calculated 5^2 as $5 \cdot 2$ and added this product to the square of 8.

2. Students simplify radicals and find their sum. If a student selects answer choice B, the student added unlike radicals. If a student selects answer choice C, he or she likely simplified $8\sqrt{2}$ as $16\sqrt{6}$ and added unlike radicals. If a student selects answer choice D, the student incorrectly simplified $8\sqrt{12}$ as $8 \cdot 4\sqrt{3}$.

Constructed Response

3. Students solve a radical equation. Students should square each side of the equation correctly to find $(x + 2)^2 = x^2 + 4x + 4$. Then students will see that in order to find the value of x, they must use completing the square or the quadratic formula.

Extended Response

4. Students will rewrite the Pythagorean Theorem for the length of a leg. For part (a), caution students to begin with the equation $d^2 = 3^2 + a^2$ and solve for a. For part (b), students should substitute 5 for d in the equation they found for part (a). For part (c), have students consider negative values for a.

Common Core Standards Practice

Week 27

Selected Response

1. What is the value of x?

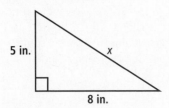

A $\sqrt{26}$ in.

B $2\sqrt{13}$ in.

C $\sqrt{74}$ in.

D $\sqrt{89}$ in.

2. What is the simplified form of $8\sqrt{12} + 3\sqrt{3}$?

A $19\sqrt{3}$

B $11\sqrt{15}$

C $19\sqrt{6}$

D $35\sqrt{3}$

Constructed Response

3. What are the solutions of
$\sqrt{9x + 1} = x + 2$?

Extended Response

4. The length of side d can be expressed as $d = \sqrt{3^2 + a^2}$.

a. Write an equation that represents the length of side a in terms of d.

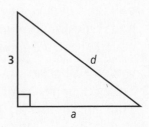

b. If $d = 5$, what are all possible values of a?

c. Are any of the values you found in part (b) extraneous solutions? Explain.

OVERVIEW

Looking Back	Mathematics of the Week	Looking Ahead
In Chapter 5, students graphed absolute value functions, in which they used the values of h and k to translate $y = |x|$ to $y = |x - h| + k$ (F.IF.C.7.b). In lesson 10-4, students solved radical equations (A.REI.2).	Students graph radical functions, including translating horizontally and vertically and stretching and shrinking.	In Algebra 2, students will graph square root and cubic functions (F.IF.C.7.b) and use translations to graph conic sections (G.GPE.A.3).

COMMON CORE MATHEMATICAL CONTENT STANDARDS

F.IF.C.7.b Graph square root, cube root…functions.

F.BF.B.3 Identify the effect on the graph of replacing $f(x)$ by $f(x) + k$, $k f(x)$, $f(kx)$, and $f(x + k)$ for specific values of k (both positive and negative)….

Also **A.CED.A.2, A.REI.A.2, F.IF.A.2**.

Common Core Mathematical Practice Standards: 1, 2, 4, 7
Materials: Graphing calculator

TEACHING NOTES

Selected Response

1. *Error Analysis*: Students translate the graph of a radical function. If a student selects answer choice B to indicate vertical stretch, the student does not recognize that the 2 in the equation indicates a vertical stretch by a factor of 2. If a student selects answer choice C to indicate the horizontal translation, the student does not recognize that "+3" indicates the translation is to the right. If the student answers E for the vertical translation, the student does not recognize that the "– 4" indicates a translation down.

Constructed Response

2. Students graph a radical function and identify the domain and range of the function. For part (a), students should use the information in the equation to identify the horizontal and vertical shifts required to translate it. For part (b), ask students how they can use the equation and the graph of the function to find the domain and range.

Extended Response

3. Students graph a radical function and solve a radical equation to answer a real-world problem. For part (a), if students are having difficulty, suggest that they draw the graph of $d = \sqrt{h}$, then graph $d = 6\sqrt{h}$, and then translate this graph to sketch the equation shown. For part (b), students should realize that they must substitute 27 for d in the function and solve the resulting radical equation. Recommend that students compare their graph to one made on a graphing calculator.

Common Core Standards Practice   Week 28

Selected Response

1. Which steps transform the graph of $y = \sqrt{x}$ to $y = 2\sqrt{x + 3} - 4$? Select all that apply.

    A Stretch vertically by the factor 2.

    B Stretch vertically by the factor $\frac{1}{2}$.

    C Translate 3 units to the right.

    D Translate 3 units to the left.

    E Translate 4 units up.

    F Translate 4 units down.

Constructed Response

2. **a.** Graph the function $y = \sqrt{x + 5} - 3$.

    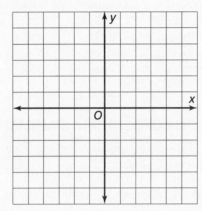

    b. What are the domain and range of the function?

Extended Response

3. The distance a person can see through a particular submarine periscope is given by the equation $d = 6\sqrt{h - 4} + 3$, where h is the height in feet above water.

    a. Graph the equation.

    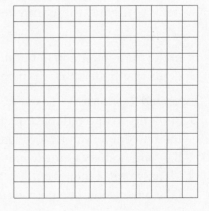

    b. How high would the submarine periscope have to be to spot a ship 27 mi away?

OVERVIEW

Looking Back	Mathematics of the Week	Looking Ahead
In Chapter 8, students multiplied binomials and factored polynomials (A.APR.A.1). In earlier lessons in this chapter, students multiplied, divided, and simplified rational expressions (A.APR.D.7).	Students divide polynomials. Students use rational functions to model real-world situations. Students identify asymptotes in the graphs of rational functions.	In Algebra 2, students will find the inverse of a function (F.BF.B.4.a) and identify holes of a rational function by factoring (A.APR.B.3).

COMMON CORE CONTENT STANDARDS

A.APR.D.6 Rewrite simple rational expressions in different forms; write $a(x)/b(x)$ in the form $q(x) + r(x)/b(x)$, where $a(x)$, $b(x)$, $q(x)$, and $r(x)$ are polynomials....

A.CED.A.2 Create equations in two or more variables to represent relationships....

F.IF.B.4 For a function...interpret key features of graphs....

F.IF.C.8.a ...show zeros, extreme values,...and interpret these in terms of a context.

Also **A.CED.A.4, F.IF.A.2**.

Common Core Mathematical Practice Standards: 1, 2, 4, 6, 7
Materials: Graphing calculator

TEACHING NOTES

Selected Response

1. *Error Analysis*: Students divide a polynomial expression by another polynomial expression. If a student selects answer choice A, he or she made a sign error. If a student selects answer choices B or D, he or she may have ignored some coefficients.

Constructed Response

2. Students must determine whether functions have asymptotes at given lines. Ask students to identify the asymptotes for each equation. For the function with equation
$y = \dfrac{(x + 2)}{(x + 2)(x - 3)} + 4$, encourage students to consider what having two factors the same in the numerator and denominator will do to the graph of the function. Suggest that students graph the functions using a graphing calculator to confirm their answers.

Extended Response

3. Students write a rational equation to solve a real-world problem. Since the problem asks them to find how long it will take Bill to complete the job alone, for part (a) ask students to relate Andrew's time working alone in terms of Bill's time. For part (b), students should identify one of their solutions as extraneous and the other as the number of days it would take Bill to complete the roofing job alone.

Common Core Standards Practice   Week 29

Selected Response

1. The length of a rectangle is $3x^2 + 5x + 2$ units and the area is $12x^3 + 23x^2 + 13x + 2$ square units. Write an expression for the width of the rectangle.

   A $4x - 1$ units

   B $x + 4$ units

   C $4x + 1$ units

   D $x - 4$ units

Constructed Response

2. Classify the following equations for those that have $y = 4$ or $x = 6$ as asymptotes of their graphs and for those that have neither as asymptotes. Write each equation in the appropriate column in the table below. Some may belong in more than one column.

$$y - 4 = \frac{1}{x - 6} \qquad y = \frac{4}{x - 6}$$

$$4y = \frac{1}{x + 6} \qquad y = \frac{(x + 2)}{(x + 2)(x - 3)} + 4$$

Graphs With $y = 4$ as Asymptote	Graphs With $x = 6$ as Asymptote	Graphs With Neither $y = 4$ nor $x = 6$ as Asymptotes

Extended Response

3. Andrew and Bill, working together, can cover the roof of a house in 6 days. Andrew, working alone, can complete the job in 5 days less than Bill. How long will it take Bill to complete the job?

   a. Write and solve a quadratic function to model this situation.

   b. Interpret your results in the context of this situation.

OVERVIEW

Looking Back	Mathematics of the Week	Looking Ahead
In Grade 6 students found the median of a set of data and in Grades 6 and 7, students developed found the mean of a set of data (6.SP.B.5.c). In Grade 6, students graphed histograms (6.SP.B.4).	Students use histograms to show the frequencies of related data. Students find the measures of central tendency and use the best measure to describe the set of data. Students make and interpret box-and-whisker plots.	In Algebra 2, students will analyze the variance of real-world data using standard deviation (S.ID.A.4).

COMMON CORE CONTENT STANDARDS

S.ID.A.2 Use statistics appropriate to the shape of the data distribution to compare center (median, mean) and spread (interquartile range, standard deviation)....

S.ID.A.3 Interpret differences in shape, center, and spread in the context of the data....

S.ID.B.5 Summarize categorical data for two categories in two-way frequency tables. Interpret relative frequencies in the context of the data....

Common Core Mathematical Practice Standards: 1, 2, 6, 7
Materials: Graphing calculator

TEACHING NOTES

Selected Response

1. *Error Analysis*: Students show understanding of vocabulary about the shape of data. If a student selects answer choice A, have the student compare choices A and C and choose the better of the two choices. If a student selects answer choices B or D, the student does not understand the term "uniform."

Constructed Response

2. The students find the mean, median, mode, and range of data and determine whether mean, median, or mode best describes the data. For part (a), ask students to define each term. You can suggest that students use a graphing calculator to find the mean and to organize the data. For part (b), ask students to justify their choice.

Extended Response

3. Students analyze a table of values representing a real-world situation, comparing data points using ratios and percents. For each part, have students write a word expression and below it write the values from the table they will need to use to answer the question. As students write each ratio as a percent, remind students that they can round their answer to a place that seems reasonable for the situation.

Common Core Standards Practice   Week 30

Selected Response

1. Which histogram is uniform?

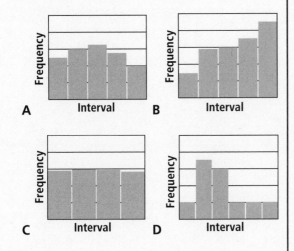

A   B

C   D

Constructed Response

2. The hours that a school band practiced per week are listed below.

   7 5 9 7 4 6 10 8 5 7 8 7 3 12 15 13 8

   a. What are the mean, median, mode, and range of their practice times?

   b. Which measure of central tendency best describes their practice times? Justify your answer.

Extended Response

3. The table below shows a company's automobile sales for the first two quarters of the year.

Quarter	Mini Buggy	Overhaul 4 ×4
1	108	216
2	198	140

Calculate the ratio and percent for each of the following situations.

a. Mini Buggy sales in quarter 1 to all Mini Buggy sales

b. Mini Buggy sales in quarter 1 to Mini Buggy sales in quarter 2

c. Overhaul 4 × 4 sales in quarter 2 to all Overhaul 4 × 4 sales

d. Overhaul 4 × 4 sales in quarter 1 to all automobile sales in both quarters

e. Which automobile's sales were highest in quarter 1? In quarter 2?

Common Core Readiness Assessment 1

1. The fare for a taxi cab is a $2 flat fee plus an additional $1.50 for each mile. Which equation represents the total cab fare in dollars?

   A $y + 2 = 1.5x$; y represents miles traveled, x represents the total fare

   B $y = 1.5x + 2$; y represents the total fare, x represents miles traveled

   C $1.5y = x + 2$; y represents the total fare, x represents miles traveled

   D $y = (1.5 + 2)x$; y represents miles traveled, x represents the total fare

2. Jimmy's age is one year less than the sum of the ages of his siblings Serena and Tyler. Which equation represents Jimmy's age?

   F $z = x + y - 1$; x represents Tyler's age, y represents Serena's age, and z represents Jimmy's age

   G $x = y + z + 1$; x represents Jimmy's age, y represents Tyler's age, and z represents Serena's age

   H $x = 1 - y + z$; x represents Serena's age, y represents Jimmy's age, and z represents Tyler's age

   J $y = x + z - 1$; x represents Jimmy's age, y represents Serena's age, and z represents Tyler's age

3. Which of the following ordered pairs is not a solution to the equation represented by the graph?

   A $(-3, 3)$
   B $(3, 0)$
   C $(0, 3)$
   D $(3, 3)$

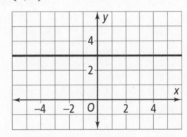

4. Which of the following reasons explains why the sum of $\frac{1}{3} + \frac{\sqrt{16}}{3}$ is a rational number?

F Since $\frac{1}{3}$ and $\frac{\sqrt{16}}{3}$ both have terminating decimals when written in decimal form, their sum is a rational number.

G A rational number is any number that can be graphed on a number line. Since $\frac{1}{3}$ and $\frac{\sqrt{16}}{3}$ can both be graphed on a number line, their sum is a rational number.

H Rational numbers are whole numbers along with their opposites. Since $\frac{1}{3}$ is the opposite of the whole number 3, and $\frac{\sqrt{16}}{3}$ is the opposite of $\frac{3}{\sqrt{16}}$, their sum is a rational number.

J Both $\frac{1}{3}$ and $\frac{\sqrt{16}}{3}$ are rational numbers. Therefore, their sum is a rational number.

5. Which property should be used next in this solution process?

$3x + 2 + 3 = 7(x - 1) - 4$
$\quad 3x + 5 = 7(x - 1) - 4$

A Commutative Property of Addition
B Identity Property of Multiplication
C Associative Property of Multiplication
D Distributive Property

6. The formula for how far a moving object travels in terms of the rate, or speed at which it moves, and the travel time, or how long it is moving, is $d = rt$, where d stands for distance, r stands for rate, and t stands for time. Rearrange the quantities in this formula to give a new formula for travel time in terms of distance and rate of travel.

F $t = rd$

G $t = \dfrac{d}{r}$

H $t = \dfrac{r}{d}$

J $t = d - r$

7. A heavy plastic rectangular sheet used in constructing greenhouses has an area of 80 ft by 40 ft. The entire sheet weighs 480 pounds. What is the weight per square foot of the sheet?

A 0.15 lb/ft
B 0.15 ft^2/lb
C 0.15 ft^2/lb^2
D 0.15 lb/ft^2

8. The table below shows amounts earned for dog-walking. How much is earned for a 7-day job?

Days, x	Dollars, y
1	13
2	26
3	39
4	52

F 87
G 89
H 91
J 93

9. Which relationship is represented by the graph below?

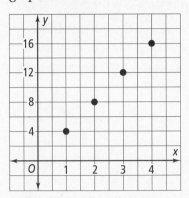

A number of quarters needed for h hours of parking if each hour costs $1

B number of hours per day Mike spends studying if he spends 30 min on each subject

C number of tickets needed for r amusement-park rides if each ride takes 6 tickets

D number of dollars collected at a car wash if each wash costs $5

10. What is the solution of $-21 = n - 8$?

F $n = -168$

G $n = -29$

H $n = -13$

J $n = 168$

11. What is the solution of $-81 = \dfrac{b}{6}$?

A $b = -486$

B $b = -75$

C $b = 13.5$

D $b = 486$

12. A gym charges $35 per month for full access to their workout equipment. Mrs. Lewis has a $140 gift certificate to the gym. For how many months can Mrs. Lewis work out using the gift certificate?

F 3 months

G 4 months

H 5 months

J 6 months

13. An auto repair shop charged $75/h for labor plus an additional $89 for parts. If the shop worked for 2 h, which equation represents the total repair cost C?

A $C = 75(2) - 89$

B $C = 89(2) + 75$

C $C = 75 + 89$

D $C = 75(2) + 89$

14. Tara works in a clothing store where she earns a base salary of $100 per day plus 12% of her daily sales. She sold $800 in clothing on Saturday and $1500 in clothing on Sunday. How much did she earn over the two days?

F $276

G $376

H $476

J $576

15. A cell phone company offers two different monthly text-messaging plans as shown in the table below. For what number of text messages will both plans cost the same?

Messaging Plan	Monthly Fee	Fee per Message
Plan A	$35.00	$0.10
Plan B	$18.00	$0.30

A 55 messages
B 85 messages
C 110 messages
D 140 messages

16. Solve the equation below for y.

$8x - 2y = 24$

F $y = 4x - 12$
G $y = 12 - 4x$
H $y = 8x - 24$
J $y = 4x - 8$

17. The equation $2w + 5j = 60$ is used to determine the number of water bottles w and the number of juice bottles j that can be bought for $60. If you purchase 4 bottles of juice, how many bottles of water can you buy?

A 10
B 15
C 20
D 25

18. The formula for the area of a triangle is $A = \dfrac{1}{2}bh$, where b is the base of the triangle and h is the height of the triangle. What is the length of the base if the area is 22 cm^2 and the height is 8 cm?

F 4.5 cm
G 5 cm
H 5.5 cm
J 6 cm

19. Solve the proportion $\dfrac{15t}{5} = \dfrac{2t + 3}{6}$.

A 0.03
B 0.1875
C 0.0375
D 0.15

20. Two rooms in a house are similar rectangles. Room A is 12 ft by 16 ft. The longer side of Room B is 4 ft shorter than twice the length of the shorter side of Room A. What are the dimensions of the second Room B?

F 15×20
G 16×20
H 16×16
J 14×16

21. A map has a scale of 1 in. : 25 mi. Two cities are 175 mi apart. How far apart are they on the map?

A 3 in.
B 5 in.
C 6 in.
D 7 in.

Common Core Readiness Assessment 2

1. A marketing consultant produced the following graph to show a client how many lawn mowers she could expect to sell, based on how much she spent on advertising. Considering that the consultant wants the graph to show that spending $32,000 on advertising should result in sales of 2200 lawn mowers, choose appropriate units and scales for the two axes.

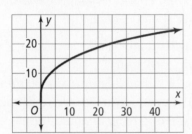

A Horizontal axis: sales, in thousands; vertical axis: dollars, in hundreds

B Horizontal axis: sales, in hundreds; vertical axis: dollars, in thousands

C Horizontal axis: dollars, in thousands; vertical axis: sales, in hundreds

D Horizontal axis: dollars, in hundreds; vertical axis: sales, in thousands

2. Which number is a solution of the inequality $4 - \frac{1}{2}b \le 33$?

    F -61
    G -60
    H -59
    J -58

3. The amount of time it would take you to go from Chicago to Las Vegas is equal to 1525 miles divided by your average rate of travel. Which equation describes how the time and rate of travel are related?

    A $y = \dfrac{1525}{x}$; x represents rate, y represents time

    B $y = 1525x$; x represents rate, y represents time

    C $y = \dfrac{x}{1525}$; x represents time, y represents rate

    D $\dfrac{y}{x} = 1525$; x represents time, y represents rate

4. Solve the inequality $-x + 6 > -(2x + 4)$.

    F $x > -10$
    G $x > -2$
    H $x < -10$
    J $x > 2$

5. Suppose it takes you 10 min to walk from home to school at a rate of 264 ft/min. Your friend lives closer to school than you do. Which inequality represents the distance d (in feet) that your friend lives from school?

    A $d < 264$
    B $d > 264$
    C $d > 2640$
    D $d < 2640$

6. Solve the inequality and graph its solutions on a number line.

$5x + 3 < 3(x + 2)$

F $x > \dfrac{3}{2}$

<++++++++++o++++++>
−5 −4 −3 −2 −1 0 1 2 3 4 5

G $x < \dfrac{3}{2}$

<++++++++++o++++++>
−5 −4 −3 −2 −1 0 1 2 3 4 5

H $x \leq \dfrac{3}{2}$

<++++++++++●++++++>
−5 −4 −3 −2 −1 0 1 2 3 4 5

J $x \geq \dfrac{3}{2}$

<++++++++++●++++++>
−5 −4 −3 −2 −1 0 1 2 3 4 5

7. The predicted thickness of the ice covering a certain pond in January is given by the formula $T = (x - 1)^r - 2p$, where T is the thickness in centimeters. If the quantity p increases by 1, what will be the change in the predicted thickness of the ice?

A The thickness will increase by 2 cm.
B The thickness will double.
C The thickness will decrease by one half.
D The thickness will decrease by 2 cm.

8. What are the solutions of the compound inequality $4d + 1 \leq -3$ or $5d - 3 > 17$?

F $d \leq -\dfrac{1}{2}$ or $d > 4$

G $d \leq -1$ or $d > 4$

H $d \leq 1$ or $d > 4$

J $d \leq 1$ or $d > 2\dfrac{4}{5}$

9. A bicyclist has a cycle computer attached to her bicycle that shows a graph of her speed during her training rides. During her last ride, her computer produced the following graph.

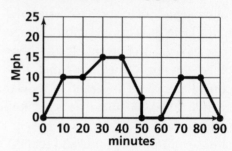

During which period(s) of time was the bicyclist's speed decreasing?

A From 40 min to 60 min and from 70 min to 90 min
B From 10 min to 20 min, from 30 min to 40 min, and from 70 min to 80 min
C From 40 min to 50 min and from 80 min to 90 min
D From 50 min to 60 min

10. Which function passes through (3, 0)?

F $y = -|x + 3|$
G $y = |x| + 3$
H $y = |x| - 3$
J $y = |x + 3|$

11. What are the solutions of $|2x + 3| > 4$?

A $x > -3\dfrac{1}{2}$ or $x > \dfrac{1}{2}$

B $x < -3\dfrac{1}{2}$ or $x > \dfrac{1}{2}$

C $x > -3\dfrac{1}{2}$ or $x < \dfrac{1}{2}$

D $x < -3\dfrac{1}{2}$ or $x > -3\dfrac{1}{2}$

12. The average gas mileage for a car is 32 mi/gal. The actual mileage may vary by at most 3 mi/gal. What are the minimum and maximum distances the car can travel on a full tank of gas if the tank's capacity is 11 gal?

F 29 mi, 35 mi

G 32 mi, 35 mi

H 319 mi, 385 mi

J 349 mi, 355 mi

13. Which of the following functions describes the sequence 1, 3, 7, 15, 31, 63, 127, ... ?

A $f(1) = 1, f(n) = f(n - 1) + n$ for $n > 1$.

B $f(1) = 1, f(n) = 2n + 1$ for $n > 1$.

C $f(1) = 1, f(n) = f(n - 1) + 2(n - 1)$ for $n > 1$.

D $f(1) = 1, f(n) = 2f(n - 1) + 1$ for $n > 1$.

14. Wanting to cut down his television-watching time slowly, Vince decides to watch 30 fewer minutes of television each week after the first. If Vince watches 6 hours of television during the first week, which of the following equations predicts Vince's hours of television n weeks after the first?

F $T(n) = 6 - 0.5n$

G $T(n) = 6n - 0.5$

H $T(n) = 6(n - 0.5)$

J $T(n) = n(6 - 0.5n)$

15. Write a formula to describe the sequence $\frac{2}{3}, 1, \frac{4}{3}, \frac{5}{3}, 2, \frac{7}{3}, ...$

A $A(n) = \frac{2}{3} + \frac{n}{3}$

B $A(n) = \frac{1}{3} + \frac{2}{3}(n - 1)$

C $A(n) = \frac{n - 1}{3}$

D $A(n) = \frac{2}{3} + (n - 1)\frac{1}{3}$

16. The graph below shows where the two functions $y = f(x)$ and $y = g(x)$ intersect. Solve the equation $f(x) = g(x)$.

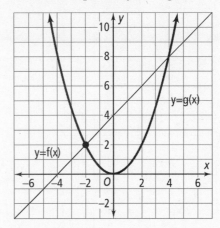

F $-2, 2, 4, 8$

G $2, 8$

H $-2, 2, 0, 4, 8$

J $-2, 4$

17. Andre rents beach chairs and umbrellas to tourists visiting the beach. On one Saturday, he has 150 customers. If he rents 125 chairs and 72 people rent both chairs and umbrellas, how many people rent umbrellas?

A 25

B 72

C 97

D 125

18. Write a formula to describe the sequence 1, 0.9, 0.8, 0.7, 0.6, 0.5....

F $A(n) = 1 - A(n - 1)$

G $A(n) = n - 0.1(n - 1)$

H $A(n) = 1 - 0.1n$

J $A(n) = 1 - 0.1(n - 1)$

19. Which is not the graph of a function?

A
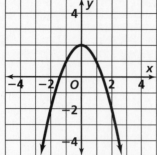

B

C
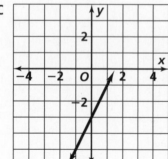

D
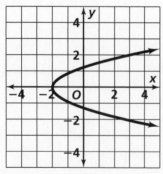

20. Determine which relation is a function.

F

x	−2	0	1	2
y	0	−2	−3	−4

G

x	0	0	0	0
y	0	1	2	3

H

x	3	3	2	0
y	1	5	5	−3

J

x	6	4	6	−1
y	0	3	2	−2

21. Which relation is not a function?

A $\{(1, -5), (2, -4), (1, -4)\}$
B $\{(1, -5), (2, -4), (3, -3)\}$
C $\{(1, -5), (2, -4), (3, 2)\}$
D $\{(1, -5), (2, -4), (3, -4)\}$

22. Which function describes the table of values?

x	2	0	2	4
f(x)	5	1	3	7

F $f(x) = 1 - 2x$
G $f(x) = 2x - 1$
H $f(x) = 3x + 1$
J $f(x) = x - 4$

23. A catalog-printing company receives a total cost C for each print job, which includes a set-up charge S and $0.05 per page p for each job. What function rule describes the situation?

A $C = 0.05p$
B $C = S + 0.05p$
C $C = 0.05S + p$
D $C = 0.05(S + p)$

24. A mountain climber is at a height of 750 m and begins his descent. He descends at a rate of 15 m/min. Which function rule describes the climber's height of elevation after t min?

F $H = 750t - 15$

G $H = 750t + 15$

H $H = 750(15t)$

J $H = 750 - 15t$

25. What is the function rule for the table below?

x	1	2	3	4
y	10	15	20	25

A $f(x) = 5x - 5$

B $f(x) = -5x - 5$

C $f(x) = -5x + 5$

D $f(x) = x - 5$

26. What is the function rule for the graph below?

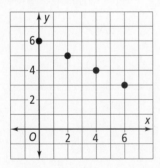

F $f(x) = -\dfrac{1}{2}x + 6$

G $f(x) = -2x + 6$

H $f(x) = -\dfrac{1}{2}x + 5$

J $f(x) = \dfrac{1}{2}x + 6$

27. Which graph represents the table below?

x	1	0	1
y	4	1	2

A

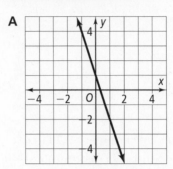

B

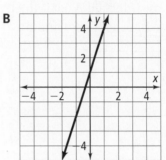

C

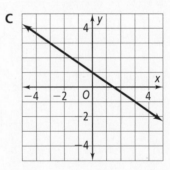

D

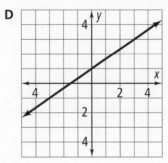

28. Suppose the average driving speed on a family trip is 48 mi/h. Which function rule models the distance traveled $d(t)$ as a function of time t spent traveling?

F $d(t) = t + 48$

G $d(t) = 48 - t$

H $d(t) = 48t$

J $d(t) = \dfrac{t}{48}$

29. An Internet café charges $2.75 to use a computer and $.35 per minute while accessing the Internet. What is the cost of using the Internet for 28 minutes?

A $2.75

B $9.80

C $10.95

D $12.55

30. The function rule $T(m) = 450 - 8m$ represents the amount of water $T(m)$ (in liters) in a holding tank after being drained at a rate of 8 L/min for m minutes. How much time has passed if there are 274 L of water in the tank?

F 18 min

G 20 min

H 22 min

J 24 min

31. The domain of $f(x)$ is $\{-1, 0, 2\}$. If $f(x) = 3x + 2$, what is the range?

A $\{-1, 0, 2\}$

B $\{-1, 2, 8\}$

C $\{-3, 0, 6\}$

D $\{-5, 32, 34\}$

Name _____ Class _____ Date _____

Common Core Readiness Assessment 2 Report

Common Core State Standards	Test Items	Number Correct	Proficient? Yes or No	Algebra 1 Student Edition Lesson(s)
Number and Quantities				
N.Q.A.1 Use units as a way to understand problems and to guide the solution of multi-step problems; choose and interpret units consistently in formulas; choose and interpret the scale and the origin in graphs and data displays.	1			4-4
N.Q.A.2 Define appropriate quantities for the purpose of descriptive modeling.	3			3-3, 4-5
Algebra				
A.SSE.A.1 Interpret expressions that represent a quantity in terms of its context. A.SSE.A.1.a Interpret parts of an expression, such as terms, factors, and coefficients.	5			4-5, 4-7
A.SSE.A.1.b Interpret complicated expressions by viewing one or more of their parts as a single entity. For example, interpret $p(1 + r)n$ as the product of p and a factor not depending on p.	7			3-7, 4-7
A.CED.A.1 Create equations and inequalities in one variable and use them to solve problems. *Include equations arising from linear and quadratic functions, and simple rational and exponential functions.*	29			3-2, 3-3, 3-4, 3-6, 3-7, 3-8
A.CED.A.2 Create equations in two or more variables to represent relationships between quantities; graph equations on coordinate axes with labels and scales.	17, 23, 24, 25			4-5
A.REI.B.3 Solve linear equations and inequalities in one variable, including equations with coefficients represented by letters.	2, 4, 6, 11			3-2, 3-3, 3-4, 3-5, 3-6
A.REI.D.10 Understand that the graph of an equation in two variables is the set of all its solutions plotted in the coordinate plane, often forming a curve (which could be a straight line).	10			4-2, 4-3, 4-4
A.REI.D.11 Explain why the x-coordinates of the points where the graphs of the equations $y = f(x)$ and $y = g(x)$ intersect are the solutions of the equation $f(x) = g(x)$; find the solutions approximately, e.g., using technology to graph the functions, make tables of values, or find successive approximations. Include cases where $f(x)$ and/or $g(x)$ are linear, polynomial, rational, absolute value, exponential, and logarithmic functions.	16			CB 4-4

Common Core Readiness Assessment 2 Report

Common Core State Standards	Test Items	Number Correct	Proficient? Yes or No	Algebra 1 Student Edition Lesson(s)
Algebra				
F.IF.A.1 Understand that a function from one set (called the domain) to another set (called the range) assigns to each element of the domain exactly one element of the range. If f is a function and x is an element of its domain, then $f(x)$ denotes the output of f corresponding to the input x. The graph of f is the graph of the equation $y = f(x)$.	19, 20, 21, 27			4-6
F.IF.A.2 Use function notation, evaluate functions for inputs in their domains, and interpret statements that use function notation in terms of a context.	22, 28, 30, 31			4-6
F.IF.A.3 Recognize that sequences are functions, sometimes defined recursively, whose domain is a subset of the integers. *For example, the Fibonacci sequence is defined recursively by $f(0) = f(1) = 1, f(n + 1) = f(n) + f(n - 1)$ for $n \geqslant 1$.*	13			4-7
F.IF.B.4 For a function that models a relationship between two quantities, interpret key features of graphs and tables in terms of the quantities, and sketch graphs showing key features given a verbal description of the relationship. Key features include: intercepts; intervals where the function is increasing, decreasing, positive, or negative; relative maximums and minimums; symmetries; end behavior; and periodicity.	9			4-2, 4-3
F.IF.B.5 Relate the domain of a function to its graph and, where applicable, to the quantitative relationship it describes. *For example, if the function h(n) gives the number of person-hours it takes to assemble n engines in a factory, then the positive integers would be an appropriate domain for the function.*	12			4-4
F.BF.A.1.a Determine an explicit expression, a recursive process, or steps for calculation from a context.	14			4-7
F.BF.A.2 Write arithmetic and geometric sequences both recursively and with an explicit formula, use them to model situations, and translate between the two forms.	15			4-7
F.LE.A.2 Construct linear and exponential functions, including arithmetic and geometric sequences, given a graph, a description of a relationship, or two input-output pairs (include reading these from a table).	26			4-7

Common Core Readiness Assessment 3

1. Find the slope of the line.

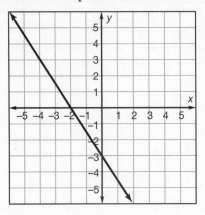

A $\dfrac{3}{2}$

B $\dfrac{2}{3}$

C $-\dfrac{2}{3}$

D $-\dfrac{3}{2}$

2. The graph below shows the distance and time of Roberto's car trip. Which of the following describes the relationship between Roberto's distance and time?

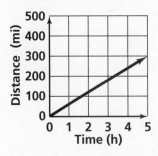

F For each hour Roberto travels, his distance increases by 100.

G Roberto's distance traveled is 5 hours divided by his speed.

H Roberto's distance is 60 times his travel time.

J Roberto traveled 300 mi.

3. What is the graph of the equation $y = 2x + 3$?

A
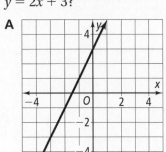

B
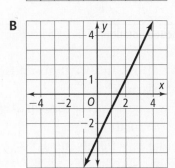

C
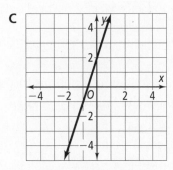

D
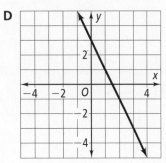

4. The following graph shows the changing ticket sales for a musical in the time after its premier. Considering that approximately 35,000 tickets were sold on the fifth weekend after release, choose scales and units for the two axes.

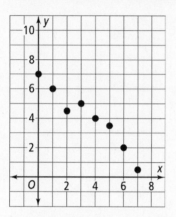

F Horizontal axis: tickets (thousands); vertical axis: weeks

G Horizontal axis: weeks; vertical axis: tickets (tens of thousands)

H Horizontal axis: tickets (tens of thousands); vertical axis: weeks

J Horizontal axis: weeks; vertical axis: tickets (thousands)

5. Which of the following functions has the same graph as the function $y = 3x + 7$?

A $-2y = 3(-2x) + 7$

B $y - 2 = 3(x - 2) + 7$

C $-2y = -6x - 14$

D $y = 3(x - 2) - 5$

6. What is the slope-intercept form of the equation $3y - 8x = 12$?

F $y = 8x + 12$

G $y = \dfrac{3}{8}x + 4$

H $y = \dfrac{8}{3}x + 4$

J $y = \dfrac{8}{3}x - 4$

7. Dieter's new pedometer measures distance as he walks. To test the accuracy of the pedometer, Dieter walks from school to his favorite restaurant, a trip he knows to be 427.4 meters long. If the reading on the pedometer says that the distance between the two places is 426 meters, what is the percent error? Round to the nearest tenth of a percent.

A 0.1%

B 0.3%

C 1.1%

D 1.4%

8. Jeremy walks into a video arcade with a pocketful of quarters. He spends them at a rate of four every quarter hour until he runs out. If the amount of quarters Jeremy has is graphed over time, which feature of the graph corresponds to Jeremy's initial amount of quarters, before he spends the first one?

F The y-intercept

G The slope

H The x-intercept

J The minimum value

9. Find the line of best fit for the following data.

x	1	4	7	9
y	0.9	2.8	3.7	4.6

A $y = 0.446x + 0.657$

B $y = 0.418x + 1.423$

C $y = 0.402x + 0.371$

D $y = 0.463x + 0.438$

10. What is the graph of the equation $y + 1 = 2(x + 2)$?

F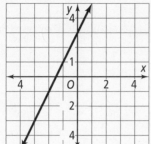

G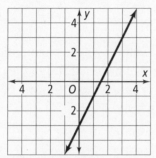

H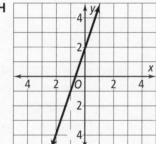

J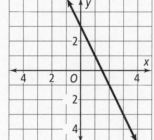

11. Find the line of best fit for the data in the following scatter plot.

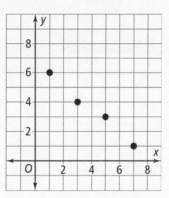

A $y = -1.2x + 8.3$

B $y = -0.6x + 8.1$

C $y = -0.4x + 7.2$

D $y = -0.8x + 6.7$

12. The changing speed of a car is modeled by the function $S(t) = -35t + 30$, where t is time in seconds. Interpret the model.

F The car has an initial speed of 0 units and is speeding up to a speed of 30 units by 35 units per second.

G The car has an initial speed of 35 units and is speeding up by 30 units per second.

H The car has an initial speed of 30 units and is slowing down by 35 units per second.

J The car has an initial speed of 30 units and is speeding up by 35 units per second.

13. Find the correlation coefficient of the line of best fit for the data in the table.

x	10	20	30	40
y	12	9.6	8.1	6.5

A -0.9985

B -0.9936

C 0.9985

D 0.9936

14. The population of a certain type of moth in an area of woodland is approximated by the formula $P = 4r - (T - 14)^2$, where r is the average monthly precipitation, T is the temperature in degrees Celsius, and P is the population of moths in tens of thousands. Which of the following conditions will result in the highest moth population?

F Temperatures close to 14°C, average rainfall close to 18 cm

G Temperatures close to 8°C, average rainfall close to 18 cm

H Temperatures close to 22°C, average rainfall close to 14 cm

J Temperatures close to 14°C, average rainfall close to 12 cm

15. Which function is shown in the following graph?

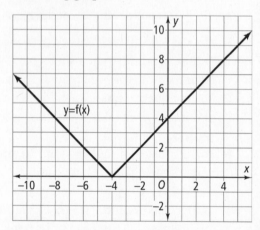

$y = f(x)$

A $f(x) = |x| + 4$
B $f(x) = |x - 4|$
C $f(x) = |x + 4|$
D $f(x) = |x| - 4$

16. What is the standard form of the equation $y = -x - 2$?

F $x + y = -2$
G $x - y = -2$
H $x + y = 2$
J $x - y = 2$

17. Which equation has a graph that is perpendicular to the graph of

$$y = -\frac{2}{3}x + 32?$$

A $y + \frac{3}{2}x = 32$

B $y + \frac{2}{3}x = 32$

C $y + 32 = -\frac{3}{2}x$

D $y - \frac{3}{2}x = 32$

18. Which of the following is an equation of the line that passes through the point $(2, 2)$ and is parallel to the graph of the equation $y = 3x - 1$?

F $y = 3x + 4$
G $y = 3x - 4$
H $y = 3x + 1$
J $y = 3x + 2$

19. Which of the following is an equation of the line that passes through the point $(-1, 4)$ and is perpendicular to the equation of the graph of $y = 4x - 3$?

A $y = -\frac{1}{4}x + \frac{17}{4}$

B $y = -\frac{1}{4}x + \frac{15}{4}$

C $y = -\frac{1}{4}x - \frac{15}{4}$

D $y = -4x + 3$

20. What is the solution of the system of linear equations in the graph shown?

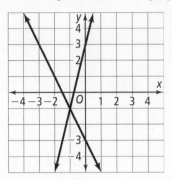

F $(-1, -1)$
G $(1, -1)$
H $(0, 1)$
J $(-1, 1)$

21. How many solutions does the system of equations shown below have?

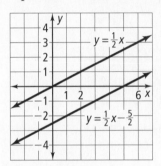

A zero solutions
B one solution
C two solutions
D infinitely many solutions

22. A recent survey of businesses found that companies with larger gross revenues typically spend more on transportation costs. What does the survey suggest about the relationship between these two quantities?

F Causation, without correlation
G Correlation, without causation
H Correlation, with causation
J Neither correlation nor causation

23. Explain why the two equations below have the same solutions.

$x + 3y = -1$
$-2x - 6y = 2$

A The two equations have the same slope, so they have the same solutions.
B The second equation is a multiple of the first equation, so they have the same solutions.
C The graphs of the equations are parallel and do not intersect, so any solution of one is a solution of the other.
D The lines are perpendicular, so they have the same solutions.

24. Suppose you have 20 coins that total $4.00. Some coins are nickels and some are quarters. Which of the following pairs of equations would you use to find out how many of each coin you have?

F $n + q = 4$
   $5n + 25q = 20$
G $n + q = 20$
   $n + q = 4.00$
H $n + q = \dfrac{4.00}{20}$
   $0.5n + 0.25q = 4.00$
J $n + q = 20$
   $5n + 25q = 400$

25. Rita is saving up $15,000 to put a down payment on a condominium. If she starts with $8000 saved and saves an additional $850 each month, which equation represents how far Rita is from her goal of reaching $15,000 saved? Let x stand for months and y stand for dollars.

A $y = 7000 - 850x$
B $y = 15,000x - 850$
C $y = 850x - 7000$
D $y = 850x + 7000$

26. A sandwich shop sells a foot-long grinder for $8 and a calzone for $6. Which equation shows the relationship between the amount of each type of product sold and the total sales, in dollars?

   F $14(x + y) = z$; x represents calzones sold; y represents grinders sold; z represents total sales

   G $6x + 8y = z$; x represents calzones sold; y represents grinders sold; z represents total sales

   H $14(x + y) = z$; x represents grinders sold; y represents calzones sold; z represents total sales

   J $6x + 8y = z$; x represents grinders sold; y represents calzones sold; represents total sales

27. Last week Reba's Reptile Store received $1975 for selling 35 reptiles. Iguanas sell for $75 and corn snakes sell for $25. How many iguanas did Reba's sell?

   A 13 iguanas

   B 17 iguanas

   C 20 iguanas

   D 22 iguanas

28. Compare the line passing through the points $(-3, -11)$ and $(6, 4)$ to the line given by the equation $y = \dfrac{3}{5}x - 6$.

   F They have the same slope.

   G They have the same x-intercept.

   H The two lines are perpendicular.

   J They have the same y-intercept.

29. Which inequality represents the graph below?

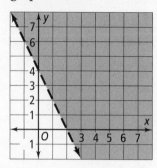

   A $y > -2x + 4$

   B $y > -2x + 2$

   C $y < -2x + 4$

   D $y > 2x + 4$

30. Which inequality represents the graph below?

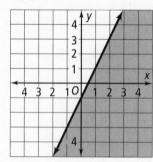

   F $y \le 2x - 1$

   G $y \le 2x + \dfrac{1}{2}$

   H $y \le -2x - 1$

   J $y < 2x - 1$

Common Core Readiness Assessment 3 Report

Common Core State Standards	Test Items	Number Correct	Proficient? Yes or No	Algebra 1 Student Edition Lesson(s)
Number and Quantities				
N.Q.A.1 Use units as a way to understand problems and to guide the solution of multi-step problems; choose and interpret units consistently in formulas; choose and interpret the scale and the origin in graphs and data displays.	4			5-7
N.Q.A.2 Define appropriate quantities for the purpose of descriptive modeling.	26			5-2, 5-5, 6-4
N.Q.A.3 Choose a level of accuracy appropriate to limitations on measurement when reporting quantities.	7			6-4
Algebra				
A.SSE.A.1.a Interpret parts of an expression, such as terms, factors, and coefficients.	14			5-3, 5-4
A.SSE.A.2 Use the structure of an expression to identify ways to rewrite it. For example, see $x^4 - y^4$ as $(x^2)^2 - (y^2)^2$, *thus recognizing it as a difference of squares that can be factored as* $(x^2 - y^2)(x^2 + y^2)$.	6, 16			5-3, 5-4, 5-5
A.CED.A.3 Represent constraints by equations or inequalities, and by systems of equations and/or inequalities, and interpret solutions as viable or nonviable options in a modeling context. *For example, represent inequalities describing nutritional and cost constraints on combinations of different foods.*	24			6-4, 6-5
A.REI.C.5 Prove that, given a system of two equations in two variables, replacing one equation by the sum of that equation and a multiple of the other produces a system with the same solutions.	23			6-3
A.REI.C.6 Solve systems of linear equations exactly and approximately (e.g., with graphs), focusing on pairs of linear equations in two variables.	21, 27			6-1, 6-2, 6-3, 6-4
A.REI.D.11 Explain why the x-coordinates of the points where the graphs of the equations $y = f(x)$ and $y = g(x)$ intersect are the solutions of the equation $f(x) = g(x)$; find the solutions approximately, e.g., using technology to graph the functions, make tables of values, or find successive approximations. Include cases where $f(x)$ and/or $g(x)$ are linear, polynomial, rational, absolute value, exponential, and logarithmic functions.	19			CB 6-1
A.REI.D.12 Graph the solutions to a linear inequality in two variables as a half plane (excluding the boundary in the case of a strict inequality), and graph the solution set to a system of linear inequalities in two variables as the intersection of the corresponding half-planes.	20, 29, 30			6-5, 6-6, CB 6-6

Common Core Readiness Assessment 3 Report

Common Core State Standards	Test Items	Number Correct	Proficient? Yes or No	Algebra 1 Student Edition Lesson(s)
Functions				
F.IF.B.6 Calculate and interpret the average rate of change of a function (presented symbolically or as a table) over a specified interval. Estimate the rate of change from a graph.	1			5-1
F.IF.C.7.a Graph linear and quadratic functions and show intercepts, maxima, and minima.	3, 10			5-3, 5-4, 5-5
F.IF.C.7.b Graph square root, cube root, and piecewise-defined functions, including step functions and absolute value functions.	15			5-8, CB 5-8
F.IF.C.9 Compare properties of two functions each represented in a different way (algebraically, graphically, numerically in tables, or by verbal descriptions).	28			5-5
F.BF.A.1.a Determine an explicit expression, a recursive process, or steps for calculation from a context.	25			5-3, 5-4, 5-5
F.BF.B.3 Identify the effect on the graph of replacing $f(x)$ by $f(x) + k$, $k f(x)$, $f(kx)$, and $f(x + k)$ for specific values of k (both positive and negative); find the value of k given the graphs. Experiment with cases and illustrate an explanation of the effects on the graph using technology. Include recognizing even and odd functions from their graphs and algebraic expressions for them.	5			5-3, CB 5-3, 5-4, 5-8
F.LE.A.1.b Recognize situations in which one quantity changes at a constant rate per unit interval relative to another.	2			5-1
F.LE.B.5 Interpret the parameters in a linear or exponential function in terms of a context.	33			5-3, 5-4, 5-5, 5-7
Geometry				
G.GPE.B.5 Prove the slope criteria for parallel and perpendicular lines and use them to solve geometric problems (e.g., find the equation of a line parallel or perpendicular to a given line that passes through a given point).	17, 18, 19			5-6
Statistics and Probability				
S.ID.B.6.a Fit a function to the data; use functions fitted to data to solve problems in the context of the data. Use given functions or choose a function suggested by the context. Emphasize linear and exponential models.	9			5-7
S.ID.B.6.c Fit a linear function for a scatter plot that suggests a linear association.	11			5-7
S.ID.C.7 Interpret the slope (rate of change) and the intercept (constant term) of a linear model in the context of the data.	12			5-7
S.ID.C.8 Compute (using technology) and interpret the correlation coefficient of a linear fit.	13			5-7
S.ID.C.9 Distinguish between correlation and causation.	22			5-7

Common Core Readiness Assessment 4

1. What is the simplified form of $(27x^3)^{(2/3)}$?

A $3x$

B $18x^2$

C $9x^2$

D $9x$

2. What is the simplified form of $\dfrac{3x^{-3}}{(2y)^{-2}}$?

F $\dfrac{2y^2}{3x^3}$

G $\dfrac{12y^2}{x^3}$

H $12x^3y^2$

J $\dfrac{1}{12x^3y^2}$

3. What is the simplified form of $\left(\dfrac{c^{-2}d^5}{d^{-1}}\right)^0$?

A 0

B 1

C $c^{-2}d^4$

D $c^{-2}d^6$

4. What is the missing value in
$x^3y^{10} \cdot x^4y^\square = x^7y^2$?

F -8

G -5

H 5

J 8

5. What is the simplified form of $\dfrac{12x^2y^{-3}}{9x^{-3}y^5}$?

A $\dfrac{4x}{3y^2}$

B $\dfrac{4x^3}{3y^5}$

C $\dfrac{4x^5}{3y^8}$

D $\dfrac{4y^8}{3x^5}$

6. What is the simplified form of
$\dfrac{(6m^3n^{-4})^2 \cdot 16n^{17}}{9m^{21}}$?

F $\dfrac{52n}{9m^{12}}$

G $\dfrac{32n^{15}}{3m^{16}}$

H $\dfrac{22n^{33}}{m^{12}}$

J $\dfrac{64n^9}{m^{15}}$

7. Make an equation to represent the area of a square whose sides are given by the expression $x + y$.

  A $A = 2x + 2y + 2xy$
  B $A = x^2 + 2xy + y^2$
  C $A = 2(x^2 + y^2)$
  D $A = x^2 + y^2$

8. The world's population is slightly under 6.8 billion. Which of the following is a reasonable representation of the world's population?

  F 6.755×10^5
  G 6.755×10^7
  H 6.755×10^9
  J 6.755×10^{11}

9. Which of the following arguments shows why $\sqrt{x}$ may be rewritten in the form $x^{1/2}$?

  A Recall that $2\sqrt{x} = x^1$. Since $2x^{1/2} = x^{2(1/2)}$ also equals x^1, $\sqrt{x}$ must be equal to $x^{1/2}$.

  B Recall that $(\sqrt{x})^2 = x^1$. Since $(x^{1/2})^2 = x^{1/2+1/2}$ is also equal to x^1, $\sqrt{x}$ must be equal to $x^{1/2}$.

  C Recall that $(\sqrt{x})^2 = x^1$. Since $\dfrac{x}{2} = x^{1/2}$, the sum $x^{1/2} + x^{1/2}$ is also equal to x^1. Therefore, $\sqrt{x}$ must be equal to $x^{1/2}$.

  D Recall that $\sqrt{x} + \sqrt{x} = x^1$. Since $x^{1/2} + x^{1/2}$ also equals x^1, $\sqrt{x}$ must be equal to $x^{1/2}$.

10. Which of the following is the graph of $y = \dfrac{1}{2} \cdot 3^x$?

F

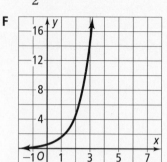

G

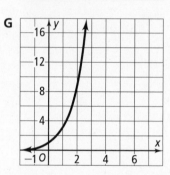

H

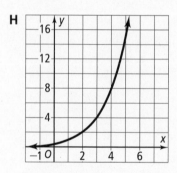

J

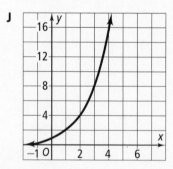

11. Which exponential function is represented by the table below?

x	0	1	3	8
y	5	10	40	1280

A $2 \cdot 5^x$

B $-5 \cdot 2^x$

C $5 \cdot 2^x$

D $5 \cdot \dfrac{1}{2}^x$

12. Evaluate the function $y = \dfrac{1}{2} \cdot 3^x$ for $x = 8$.

F 85

G 3280.5

H 6561

J 13,122

13. Which of the following statements is always true about the function $y = a \cdot b^x$?

A When $a > 0$ and $b > 1$, the function models exponential decay.

B When $a > 0$ and $b > 1$, the function models exponential growth.

C When $a > 0$ and $0 < b < 1$, the function models exponential growth.

D When $a < 0$ and $0 < b < 1$, the function models exponential decay.

14. Which of the following statements is never true?

F All quadratic trinomials can be written as the product of two binomial factors.

G Some quadratic trinomials can be written as the product of two binomial factors.

H Some quadratic trinomials have a greatest common factor.

J Some quadratic trinomials have binomial factors that are the same.

15. An investment grows according to the exponential equation $y = 15{,}000 \cdot 1.07^x$, where x is the number of years invested. Which of the following statements is true?

A The investment will continue to grow at a rate of 7% per year compounded quarterly.

B The investment will increase by $1050 per year.

C The investment will more than double within 12 years.

D The investment will triple within 15 years.

16. What is the simplified form of
$5x + 6 - 4x^2 + 3x$?

   F $4x^2 + 8x + 6$

   G $4x^2 + 2x + 6$

   H $-4x^2 + 8x + 6$

   J $-4x^2 + 2x + 6$

17. Add:

$(7x^2 - 8x^3 + 4) + (9x^3 + 2x^2 + 7)$

   A $-x^3 + 9x^2 + 11$

   B $16x^5 - 6x + 11$

   C $x^3 + 9x^2 + 11$

   D $x^3 + 9x^2 - 3$

18. Subtract:

$(x^2 + 6x - 8) - (-3x^2 + 2x - 9)$

   F $4x^2 + 4x + 1$

   G $-2x^2 + 4x + 1$

   H $4x^2 + 4x + 17$

   J $4x^2 + 8x + 17$

19. If the perimeter of a triangle is $10x + 5y$ and two of the sides are $3x + 4y$ and $5x - y$, which is the third side?

   A $2x + 2y$

   B $2x + y$

   C $-2x + 2y$

   D $x + 2y$

20. What is the simplified form of
$(-5a^2 + 6a + 2) - (3a^2 - 4a - 5)$?

   F $-8a^2 + 10a + 7$

   G $-8a^2 + 2a + 7$

   H $-2a^2 + 10a + 7$

   J $-8a^2 + 10a - 3$

21. What is the simplified form of
$(3b^2 - 8) + (5b + 9) - (b^2 + 6b - 4)$?

   A $4b^2 + 11b - 13$

   B $4b^2 - b + 5$

   C $2b^2 - b + 5$

   D $2b^2 + b - 13$

22. Write the explicit formula for the geometric sequence 324, 108, 36, 12, 4, ...

   F $\left(\dfrac{324}{2}\right)^{n-1}$

   G $4 \cdot 3^{n-1}$

   H $324 \cdot \left(\dfrac{1}{3}\right)^{n-1}$

   J $324 - 3^{n-1}$

23. An engineer uses the equation $y = -0.2x + 0.8$ to model the data in the following table.

x	0	1	2	3	4
y	1	0.5	0.25	0.125	0.0625

Find the elements of the domain for which the engineer's model predicts a higher value of y than the actual value.

   A $\{1, 2, 3\}$

   B $\{2, 3\}$

   C $\{0, 4\}$

   D $\{1, 2, 3, 4\}$

24. The width of a box is 1 cm less than its length. The height of the box is 9 cm greater than the length. The dimensions can be represented by $x, x - 1$, and $x + 9$. Multiply the dimensions and find the greatest common factor of the terms.

   F x^4

   G x^3

   H x^2

   J x

25. Compare the graphs of the two functions $f(x) = 2^x$, and $g(x)$. Determine the equation of $g(x)$.

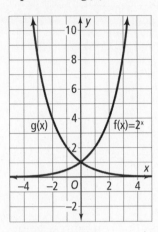

A $g(x) = -2^x$

B $g(x) = (-2)^x$

C $g(x) = 2^{-x}$

D $g(x) = \left(\dfrac{1}{2}\right)^{-x}$

26. What is the factored form of $x^2 + 3x - 70$?

F $(x + 7)(x - 10)$

G $(x + 15)(x - 4)$

H $(x - 7)(x + 10)$

J $(x + 7)(x - 4)$

27. A circle's area is represented by $A = \pi(x^2 - 22x + 121)$. What expression represents the radius of the circle?

A $x + 11$

B $x - 11$

C $x - 22$

D $x + 22$

28. What is the factored form of $5d^2 + 6d - 8$?

F $(5d - 2)(d + 4)$

G $(5d + 4)(d + 2)$

H $(5d - 4)(d + 2)$

J $(5d - 4)(d - 2)$

29. What is the factored form of $49b^2 - 56b + 16$?

A $(4b - 7)^2$

B $(7b - 4)^2$

C $(7b - 8)(7b - 2)$

D $(8b - 7)(2b - 7)$

30. The area of a rectangle is $10r^2 - 11r - 6$. The width is $2r - 3$. What is the length?

F $8r - 3$

G $5r + 2$

H $5r + 3$

J $5r - 2$

31. Which function best models the sequence 2, 4, 8, 16, 32, ... ?

A $A(n) = 2n$

B $A(n) = 2^n$

C $A(n) = n^2$

D $A(n) = n^2 + 1$

32. Factor $10x^2 + 19x + 6$ by grouping.

F $(5x + 2)(2x + 3)$

G $(x + 2)(10x + 3)$

H $2(x + 1)(5x + 3)$

J $2(5x + 1)(x + 3)$

33. An analyst predicts that the demand for homeowner's insurance will continue to decline for a time, and then begin to climb. Her model for the number of insurance policies demanded, shown in the following graph, is $D = 0.0625t^2 - 0.75\,t + 4.25$, where D represents tens of millions of policies and t is time in months. On what interval does the analyst predict that the demand for policies will increase?

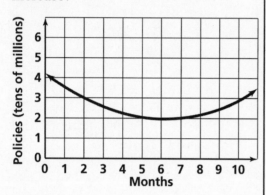

A $t \geqslant 6$
B $4 \leqslant t \leqslant 10$
C $t \geqslant 8$
D $0 \leqslant t \leqslant 6$

34. The function $b(h)$ models the percent of a certain wildflower that blooms during months in which the average daily sunlight is h hours. Name the most appropriate domain for this function.

F Integers, $h \leqslant 24$
G Integers, $0 \leqslant h \leqslant 24$
H Real numbers, $0 \leqslant h \leqslant 24$
J Whole numbers, $h \leqslant 24$

35. What is the width of the rectangle shown below?

$5x + 1$

$A = 10x^2 - 13x - 3$

A $x - 3$
B $2x - 5$
C $2x - 3$
D $2x - 1$

36. Which expressions can represent the dimensions of a rectangular prism with a volume of $12y^3 + 62y^2 + 80y$?

F $2y, 2y + 8, 3y + 5$
G $2y, 2y + 4, 3y + 10$
H $y, 2y + 5, 3y + 8$
J $2y, 2y + 5, 3y + 8$

37. An experimental machine heats up rapidly as it operates. Engineers measure its temperature every 10 seconds and record the results in a table.

time (seconds)	0	10	20	30	40
temperature (°C)	20.000	24.000	28.800	34.560	41.472

Describe how the temperature of the machine changes over time.

A The temperature increases by 20% every 10 seconds.
B The temperature increases by $0.4t°$C where t is the time in seconds.
C The temperature doubles every 40 seconds.
D The temperature increases by 4°C every 10 seconds.

Common Core Readiness Assessment 4 Report

Algebra 1 Concepts	Test Items	Number Correct	Proficient? Yes or No	Algebra 1 Student Edition Lesson(s)
Number and Quantities				
N.RN.A.1 Explain how the definition of the meaning of rational exponents follows from extending the properties of integer exponents to those values, allowing for a notation for radicals in terms of rational exponents.	9			7-2, 7-3, 7-4
N.RN.A.2 Rewrite expressions involving radicals and rational exponents using the properties of exponents.	1			7-5
Algebra				
A.SSE.A.1 Interpret expressions that represent a quantity in terms of its context. A.SSE.A.1.a Interpret parts of an expression, such as terms, factors, and coefficients.	15			7-6, 7-7, 7-8, 8-5, 8-6, 8-7, 8-8
A.SSE.A.2 Use the structure of an expression to identify ways to rewrite it. For example, see $x^4 - y^4$ as $(x^2)^2 - (y^2)^2$, thus recognizing it as a difference of squares that can be factored as $(x^2 - y^2)(x^2 + y^2)$.	30, 35			8-7, 8-8
A.SSE.B.3.c Use the properties of exponents to transform expressions for exponential functions.	2, 3, 4, 5, 6			7-7
A.APR.A.1 Understand that polynomials form a system analogous to the integers, namely, they are closed under the operations of addition, subtraction, and multiplication; add, subtract, and multiply polynomials.	14, 16, 17, 18, 20, 21, 24, 26, 28, 29, 34			8-1, 8-2, 8-3, 8-4
A.CED.A.2 Create equations in two or more variables to represent relationships between quantities; graph equations on coordinate axes with labels and scales.	7			7-6, 7-7
A.REI.D.11 Explain why the x-coordinates of the points where the graphs of the equations $y = f(x)$ and $y = g(x)$ intersect are the solutions of the equation $f(x) = g(x)$; find the solutions approximately, e.g., using technology to graph the functions, make tables of values, or find successive approximations. Include cases where $f(x)$ and/or $g(x)$ are linear, polynomial, rational, absolute value, exponential, and logarithmic functions.	12			7-6
Functions				
F.IF.A.3 Recognize that sequences are functions, sometimes defined recursively, whose domain is a subset of the integers.	31			7-8
F.IF.B.4 For a function that models a relationship between two quantities, interpret key features of graphs and tables in terms of the quantities, and sketch graphs showing key features given a verbal description of the relationship. *Key features include: intercepts; intervals where the function is increasing, decreasing, positive, or negative; relative maximums and minimums; symmetries; end behavior; and periodicity.*	32			7-6, 7-7

Name _____ Class _____ Date _____

Common Core Readiness Assessment 4 Report

Algebra 1 Concepts	Test Items	Number Correct	Proficient? Yes or No	Algebra 1 Student Edition Lesson(s)
F.IF.B.5 Relate the domain of a function to its graph and, where applicable, to the quantitative relationship it describes.	33			7-6
F.IF.C.7 Graph functions expressed symbolically and show key features of the graph, by hand in simple cases and using technology for more complicated cases. F.IF.C.7.e Graph exponential and logarithmic functions, showing intercepts and end behavior, and trigonometric functions, showing period, midline, and amplitude.	10			7-6, 7-7
F.IF.C.8 Write a function defined by an expression in different but equivalent forms to reveal and explain different properties of the function.	27			7-7
F.IF.C.8.b Use the properties of exponents to interpret expressions for exponential functions.	8			7-7
F.IF.C.9 Compare properties of two functions, each represented in a different way (algebraically, graphically, numerically in tables, or by verbal descriptions). *For example, given a graph of one quadratic function and an algebraic expression for another, say which has the larger maximum.*	23			7-6
F.BF.A.1 Write a function that describes a relationship between two quantities.	36			7-7
F.BF.A.1.a Determine an explicit expression, a recursive process, or steps for calculation from a context.	19			7-7
F.BF.A.2 Write arithmetic and geometric sequences both recursively and with an explicit formula, use them to model situations, and translate between the two forms.	22			7-8
F.BF.B.3 Identify the effect on the graph of replacing $f(x)$ by $f(x) + k$, $k f(x)$, $f(kx)$, and $f(x + k)$ for specific values of k (both positive and negative); find the value of k given the graphs. Experiment with cases and illustrate an explanation of the effects on the graph using technology. *Include recognizing even and odd functions from their graphs and algebraic expressions for them.*	25			7-8
F.LE.A.1.c Recognize situations in which a quantity grows or decays by a constant percent rate per unit interval relative to another.	37			7-7
F.LE.A.2: Construct linear and exponential functions, including arithmetic and geometric sequences, given a graph, a description of a relationship, or two input-output pairs (include reading these from a table).	11			7-6, 7-8
F.LE.B.5 Interpret the parameters in a linear or exponential function in terms of a context.	13			7-7

Common Core Readiness Assessment 5

1. Which of the following is a graph of the quadratic equation $y = x^2 - 5$?

A

B

C

D

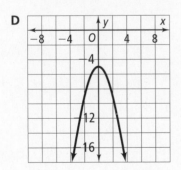
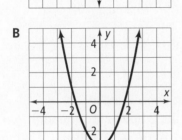

2. Which of the following is an equation of the graph shown below?

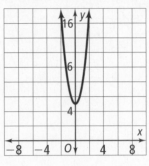

F $y = 5x^2 + 3$

G $y = 2x^2 + 5$

H $y = 3x^2$

J $y = 3x^2 + 5$

3. What is the equation of the axis of symmetry of a parabola if its x-intercepts are -3 and 7?

A $x = 1$

B $x = 2$

C $x = 3$

D $x = 4$

4. What is the domain of the graph shown below?

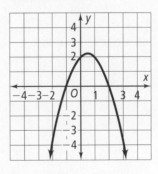

F $x \leq 2.2$

G $x \geq 2.2$

H $x \leq -1$

J all real numbers

5. What is the axis of symmetry of the function below?

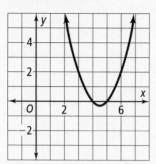

A $x = 0$

B $x = 4$

C $x = 4.5$

D $x = 5$

6. Which equation is graphed below?

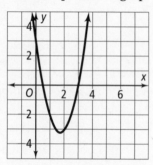

F $y = -2x^2 - 7x + 3$

G $y = 2x^2 - 7x + 3$

H $y = 2x^2 - 7x - 3$

J $y = \frac{1}{2}x^2 - 7x + 3$

7. What is the vertex of the function

$y = -\frac{3}{2}x^2 - x + 8?$

A $\left(-\frac{1}{3}, 8\right)$

B $\left(-\frac{1}{3}, \frac{49}{6}\right)$

C $\left(\frac{1}{3}, 8\right)$

D $\left(\frac{1}{3}, \frac{49}{6}\right)$

8. Which of the following equations has a graph that opens downward and has a vertex 3 units below the origin?

F $y = -2x^2 + 3$

G $y = -(3 + x^2)$

H $y = 4x^2 + 3$

J $y = (x + 4)^2$

9. Which equation has an axis of symmetry of $x = 4$?

A $y = (x + 4)^2$

B $y = x^2 - 8x + 16$

C $y = \frac{1}{2}x^2 - 8x + 8$

D $y = \frac{3}{4}x^2 + 8x + 16$

10. Find the x-coordinate of the vertex of the graph of the equation $y = -3x^2 + 10x - 9.$

F $-\frac{5}{9}$

G 3

H $-\frac{3}{2}$

J $\frac{5}{3}$

11. The graph of $y = -2x^2$ is shown below. Use the graph to determine the solution(s) to the equation $-2x^2 = 0$.

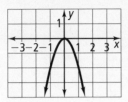

  A -1

  B 0

  C 1

  D $-1, 1$

12. What are the solutions of $2x^2 - 32 = 0$?

  F $x = \pm 3$

  G $x = \pm 4$

  H $x = \pm 5$

  J $x = \pm 6$

13. The formula for the area of a circle is $A = \pi r^2$.

If the area of a circle is represented by $A = 21\pi$, what is the radius of the circle? Round your answer to the nearest tenth.

  A $x = 10.5$

  B $x = 5$

  C $x = 4.6$

  D $x = 4.0$

14. What are the solutions of the equation $(2x + 5)(x - 4) = 0$?

  F $x = -\dfrac{5}{2}$ or $x = -4$

  G $x = -\dfrac{5}{2}$ or $x = 4$

  H $x = \dfrac{5}{2}$ or $x = -4$

  J $x = \dfrac{5}{2}$ or $x = 4$

15. What are the solutions of the equation $a^2 + 7a + 12 = 0$?

  A $a = 3$ or $a = 4$

  B $a = 3$ or $a = -4$

  C $a = -3$ or $a = 4$

  D $a = -3$ or $a = -4$

16. What are the solutions of the equation $z^2 = 18 - 7z$?

  F -9 and 2

  G -6 and 3

  H -9 and -2

  J -2 and 9

17. What are the solutions of the equation $5x^2 + 27x + 10 = 0$?

A $-\dfrac{2}{5}$ and 5

B -5 and -2

C -5 and $-\dfrac{2}{5}$

D 5 and $\dfrac{2}{5}$

18. What are the solutions of $3x^2 - 22x = -24$?

F $x = -\dfrac{4}{3}$ or $x = -6$

G $x = -\dfrac{4}{3}$ or $x = 6$

H $x = \dfrac{4}{3}$ or $x = -6$

J $x = \dfrac{4}{3}$ or $x = 6$

19. A rectangular area is being covered with concrete so a picnic table can eventually be placed on it. The concrete pad has an area of 48 ft^2. The length of the pad is 4 ft shorter than twice its width. What are the dimensions of the concrete pad?

A 4 ft by 12 ft

B 7 ft by 9 ft

C 8 ft by 6 ft

D 10 ft by 8 ft

20. What are the solutions of $2x^2 + 9x = -4$? Use the quadratic formula.

F $x = -4$ or $x = -2$

G $x = 4$ or $x = \dfrac{1}{2}$

H $x = -4$ or $x = -\dfrac{1}{2}$

J $x = 4$ or $x = 2$

21. A ball is kicked from an initial height of 2.5 feet with an initial velocity of 45 feet per second. The equation $y = -16x^2 + 45x + 2.5$ models its path, where x is the time (in seconds) of the ball travels and y is height (in feet) of the ball is kicked. How long does it take for the ball to reach the ground? Round to the nearest tenth of a second.

A $x = 2.4$

B $x = 2.6$

C $x = 2.8$

D $x = 3.0$

22. What is the number of real-number solutions of $5x^2 + 14x = 7$?

F none

G one

H two

J infinitely many

23. Make a formula to find the area of any rectangle whose length is one more than its width.

   A Area $= x + (x + 1)$; x represents length

   B Area $= x^2 + x$; x represents width

   C Area $= x^2 + 1$; x represents length

   D Area $= x(x - 1)$; x represents width

24. Choose the explanation below that proves that $x - 1 = x^2 + 1$ has no solutions.

   F The graphs of functions $f(x) = x - 1$ and $g(x) = x^2 + 1$ do not intersect.

   G The function $f(x) = x - 1$ is negative for some values of x, but the function $g(x) = x^2 + 1$ is always positive.

   H The function $f(x) = x - 1$ is a factor of the function $g(x) = x^2 + 1$.

   J The function $f(x) = x - 1$ is linear and $g(x) = x^2 + 1$ is a quadratic function.

25. The diagonal corner-to-corner distance across a square is measured to be approximately 11 meters. If the sides of the square are exactly 8 meters long, what is the percent error of the measurement? Round to the nearest tenth of a percent.

   A 1.4%

   B 4.7%

   C 7.1%

   D 2.8%

26. A biologist determined that the quantity of bacteria in a petri dish decreases by half every day of the study. If there were 8 grams of bacteria at the beginning of the study, predict how many grams will be left after 3.5 days. Round to the nearest hundredth.

   F 0.75 g

   G 1.14 g

   H 0.67 g

   J 0.71 g

27. What number c must be added to both sides of the equation $x^2 - 6x = 16$ so that it may be rewritten in the form $(x - 3)^2 = 16 + c$?

   A 36

   B -3

   C 9

   D -10

28. Find the x-coordinates of the solutions to the system of equations.

$$-x + y = 2$$
$$y = x^2 - 4$$

   F 0, 2

   G $-2, 3$

   H 2, 4

   J $-3, 0$

29. Find the domain on which the absolute value of x is greater than or equal to x^2.

    A $-1 \leq x \leq 1$

    B $x \neq 0$

    C $x \leq -1$ and $x \geq 1$

    D $0 \leq x \leq 1$

30. The cost to purchase enough of a certain fertilizer to treat a garden is \$.25 per square foot of the garden, plus \$20.00 for shipping. Write an equation describing the cost in dollars to purchase fertilizer for a garden that is 12 feet longer than it is wide. Use x to represent the width of the garden.

    F $\text{Cost} = \dfrac{1}{4}x^2 + 3x + 5$

    G $\text{Cost} = \dfrac{1}{4}x^2 + 23$

    H $\text{Cost} = \dfrac{1}{4}x^2 + 3x + 20$

    J $\text{Cost} = \dfrac{1}{4}x^2 + 10x + 20$

31. Find the sum of the linear function $f(x) = 3x - 7$ and the quadratic function $g(x) = 2x^2 - 3x + 12$.

    A $2x^2 + 6x + 19$

    B $2x^2 + 5$

    C $5x^2 + 5$

    D $2x^2 - 6x - 19$

32. What is the length of the missing side of the triangle shown below?

    F 13

    G 19

    H 169

    J 250

33. What is the domain of the function $y = 3\sqrt{x + 2}$?

    A $x \leq -2$

    B $x \geq 0$

    C $x \geq -2$

    D $x \geq 2$

34. The graph of which function is shown below?

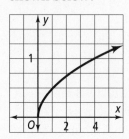

    F $y = 4\sqrt{x}$

    G $y = 2\sqrt{x}$

    H $y = \sqrt{x}$

    J $y = \dfrac{1}{2}\sqrt{x}$

35. Which of the following is true about the graph of $y = \sqrt{x - 5}$?

A The graph of $y = \sqrt{x - 5}$ is the graph of $y = \sqrt{x}$ translated 5 units up.

B The graph of $y = \sqrt{x - 5}$ is the graph of $y = \sqrt{x}$ translated 5 units to the left.

C The graph of $y = \sqrt{x - 5}$ is the graph of $y = \sqrt{x}$ translated 5 units down.

D The graph of $y = \sqrt{x - 5}$ is the graph of $y = \sqrt{x}$ translated 5 units to the right.

36. Select the argument that proves that a linear function $f(x) = mx + b$ grows by equal differences over equal intervals.

F Pick any two numbers x_1 and x_2 with $x_1 < x_2$. Then $f(x_2) - f(x_1) = m(x_2 - x_1)$. That is, f grows by the slope times the change in x.

G Pick any two numbers x_1 and x_2 with $x_1 < x_2$. Then $f(x_2) - f(x_1) = m \dfrac{x_2}{x_1}$. That is, f grows by the slope times the ratio of the values of x.

H Pick any two numbers x_1 and x_2 with $x_1 < x_2$. Then $f(x_2) - f(x_1) = m^{(x_2 - x_1)}$. That is, f grows by the slope raised to the power of the change in x.

J Pick any two numbers x_1 and x_2 with $x_1 < x_2$. Then $f(x_2) - f(x_1) = \dfrac{1}{m}(x_2 - x_1)$. That is, f grows by the change in x, divided by the slope.

37. Which function best models the data in the table?

x	0	1	2	3	4
y	100	115	132	152	175

A $f(x) = \dfrac{75}{4}x + 100$

B $f(x) = 5x^2 + 10\,0$

C $f(x) = 100 \cdot 1.15^x$

D $f(x) = \dfrac{75}{2}\sqrt{x} + 100$

38. Two economists propose models to predict the changing demand for a certain commodity over time. The first uses a quadratic model $f(t)$, and the second uses an exponential model, $g(t)$. The predictions for the first 12 months are shown in the table, rounded to the nearest hundredth. Compare the two economists' models.

Use the following table to answer #38.

t (months)	$f(t)$ (demand)	$g(t)$ (demand)
1	2.52	1.76
2	2.58	1.94
3	2.68	2.13
4	2.82	2.34
5	3.00	2.58
6	3.22	2.83
7	3.48	3.12
8	3.78	3.43
9	4.12	3.77
10	4.50	4.15
11	4.92	4.56
12	5.38	5.02

F The quadratic model grows faster than the exponential model. For large values of t, $f(t)$ will be greater than $g(t)$.

G The models have similar growth rates. For large values of t, the difference between $f(t)$ and $g(t)$ will get closer and closer to zero.

H The models have similar growth rates. For large values of t, the difference between $f(t)$ and $g(t)$ will get closer and closer to 0.3.

J The exponential model grows faster than the quadratic model. For large values of t, $g(t)$ will be greater than $f(t)$.

Common Core Readiness Assessment 5 Report

Common Core State Standards	Test Items	Number Correct	Proficient? Yes or No	Algebra 1 Student Edition Lesson(s)
Number and Quantities				
N.Q.A.2 Define appropriate quantities for the purpose of descriptive modeling.	23			9-3
N.Q.A.3 Choose a level of accuracy appropriate to limitations on measurement when reporting quantities.	25			9-5, 9-6
Algebra				
A.SSE.B.3 Choose and produce an equivalent form of an expression to reveal and explain properties of the quantity represented by the expression. A.SSE.B.3.a Factor a quadratic expression to reveal the zeros of the function it defines.	9, 16			9-4, 9-5
A.SSE.B.3.b Complete the square in a quadratic expression to reveal the maximum or minimum value of the function it defines.	10, 27			9-5
A.CED.A.3 Represent constraints by equations or inequalities, and by systems of equations and/or inequalities, and interpret solutions as viable or non-viable options in a modeling context.	19			9-8
A.CED.A.4 Rearrange formulas to highlight a quantity of interest, using the same reasoning as in solving equations.	8, 13			9-3
A.REI.B.4 Solve quadratic equations in one variable.	11, 18, 32			9-3, 9-4, 9-5, 9-6
A.REI.B.4.a Use the method of completing the square to transform any quadratic equation in x into an equation of the form $(x - p)^2 = q$ that has the same solutions. Derive the quadratic formula from this form.	12, 14, 17, 20			9-5, 9-6
A.REI.B.4.b Solve quadratic equations by inspection (e.g., for $x^2 = 49$), taking square roots, completing the square, the quadratic formula, and factoring, as appropriate to the initial form of the equation. Recognize when the quadratic formula gives complex solutions and write them as $a \pm bi$ for real numbers a and b.	15, 21, 22			9-3, 9-4, 9-5, 9-6
A.REI.C.7 Solve a simple system consisting of a linear equation and a quadratic equation in two variables algebraically and graphically.	28			9-8

Common Core Readiness Assessment 5 Report

Common Core State Standards	Test Items	Number Correct	Proficient? Yes or No	Algebra 1 Student Edition Lesson(s)
A.REI.D.11 Explain why the *x*-coordinates of the points where the graphs of the equations $y = f(x)$ and $y = g(x)$ intersect are the solutions of the equation $f(x) = g(x)$; find the solutions approximately, e.g., using technology to graph the functions, make tables of values, or find successive approximations. Include cases where $f(x)$ and/or $g(x)$ are linear, polynomial, rational, absolute value, exponential, and logarithmic functions.	24			9-8
Functions				
F.IF.B.5 Relate the domain of a function to its graph and, where applicable, to the quantitative relationship it describes.	4, 29, 33, 35			9-1
F.IF.C.8.a Use the process of factoring and completing the square in a quadratic function to show zeros, extreme values, and symmetry of the graph, and interpret these in terms of a context.	1, 2, 7			
F.BF.A.1 Write a function that describes a relationship between two quantities.	6, 30			9-2
F.BF.A.1.b Combine standard function types using arithmetic operations.	31			9-7
F.LE.A.1.a Prove that linear functions grow by equal differences over equal intervals, and that exponential functions grow by equal factors over equal intervals.	36			9-7
F.LE.A.2 Construct linear and exponential functions, including arithmetic and geometric sequences, given a graph, a description of a relationship, or two input-output pairs (include reading these from a table).	3, 5, 26, 37			9-7
F.LE.A.3 Observe using graphs and tables that a quantity increasing expoxnentially eventually exceeds a quantity increasing linearly, quadratically, or (more generally) as a polynomial function.	38			CB 9-2, 9-7
Statistics and Probability				
S.ID.B.6.a Fit a function to the data; use functions fitted to data to solve problems in the context of the data. *Use given functions or choose a function suggested by the context. Emphasize linear and exponential models.*	16			9-7

Quarter 1 Test

Chapters 1–3

Form G

Write an expression for the phrase. Use x to represent the unknown quantity.

1. With the return of the $8 deposit, the total rental fee came to $8 less than 12 times the hourly rate.

2. Write an explicit formula for the sequence given by the recursive definition $A(1) = 1$, and $A(n+1) = A(n) + 7$.

3. A manned glider is launched horizontally from a height of 100 feet. While in flight, its height above the ground in feet is given by the function $h(t) = -2t + 100$, where t is time in seconds. What is the domain of $h(t)$?

4. Name the first three numbers in the sequence.
   ___ ___ ___ 80 160 320 640 1280....

5. Name the domain of the function $\{(2,2), (3,7), (5,23), (8,62)\}$.

6. Solve: $\dfrac{x}{6} = \dfrac{5}{8}$

7. You have a coupon for 10% off of a DVD that costs $15. If a tax of 8% is charged on the original amount, what will you pay for the DVD?

8. Use an equation to model the relationship shown in the table.

Month	Cost
1	$12
2	$24
3	$36
4	$48

9. For $f(x) = \sqrt{x}$, estimate $f(68)$ to the nearest integer.

10. Which property is illustrated?
    $$(4 \cdot -7) \cdot 5 = 4(-7 \cdot 5)$$

Solve each inequality. Check your answer.

11. $n - 9.4 \geq 15.6$

12. $-20 \leq -4x$

13. The formula for finding the area of a triangle is $A = \dfrac{1}{2}bh$.
    A triangle has height 12 in. and area 54 in.^{2}. What is the length of its base?

Quarter 1 Test (continued)

Form G

Chapters 1–3

14. The following graph shows the distance over time between a car and a police officer. For how many seconds was the car within 200 feet or less of the officer?

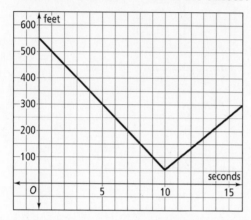

15. Which property is illustrated?

$6(3 + 1) = 6 \cdot 3 + 6 \cdot 1$

16. Write an equation to model this situation. Then use your equation to solve. Jack saved $16.50 to spend on amusement-ride tickets. Each ticket costs $0.75. How many tickets can Jack buy?

17. Is the sum $\frac{1}{3} + 0.25$ a rational number?

18. Use the graph to find the solution of $f(x) = 0$.

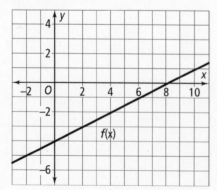

19. There are 15 clowns in a circus. Each clown has to act either happy or sad. Twelve of the clowns have red noses. Each of the seven happy clowns has a red nose. Five of the sad clowns have red noses. How many clowns have to act sad and do not have a red nose?

Solve each equation. Check your answer.

20. $9k - 2 = 43$

21. $2(y + 5) = 16$

22. $5(h + 2) = -3(4 - h)$

23. Simplify the expression.

$$\frac{88 \cdot (x^2 + y^2)}{(x^2 + y^2) \cdot 14}$$

24. Schools often have a section of street called a school zone located near their entrances. In a school zone, driving speeds are reduced at certain times of the day. If a school zone is 0.3 mi long, how many minutes longer does it take to drive through it at 20 mi/h than at 30 mi/h?

25. $\triangle CAB$ is similar to $\triangle EDF$. What is the length of $\overline{DE}$?

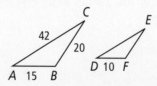

Quarter 2 Test

Form G

Chapters 4–6

Solve each system by graphing.

1. $y = -x + 5$
$y = 2x - 4$

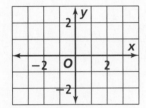

2. $y > 5x + 1$
$y \le -x + 3$

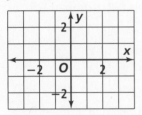

3. Solve the system using elimination.

$6x - 18y = 60$
$9x + 2y = 32$

Write a system of equations to model each situation. Solve by any method.

4. Lisa charges $25 for private tutoring and $18 for group tutoring. In one day, Lisa earned $265 from 12 students. How many students of each type did she tutor?

5. A collection of quarters and nickels is worth $1.25. There are 13 coins in all. How many of each coin are there?

6. A new animal species is introduced to an uninhabited island. The species has an abundant food source and its population thrives. Sketch a graph showing what the population of the species might look like over time.

7. Model the rule $f(x) = -\dfrac{1}{2}x + 3$ with a table and a graph.

8. The table shows a school district's enrollment for two successive years. Write a linear function using the data (with x representing the year number), and then use the model to predict the enrollment in Year 4.

Year 1	8295
Year 2	8072

9. Write an equation in point-slope form for the line through the point $(2, -7)$ with slope $m = -\dfrac{1}{3}$.

10. What is the range of the function $f(x) = x^2 + 1$, when the domain is $\{-6, 4, 8\}$?

Write a function rule to describe the statement.

11. the amount of change $c(x)$ from a $20 bill if you buy x pounds of pears for $0.79/lb

12. Write the equation of direct variation that includes the point $(14, -28)$.

Find the next three terms of the arithmetic sequence.

13. 9, 12, 15, ...   **14.** 288, 252, 216, ...

Quarter 2 Test (continued)   *Form G*

Chapters 4–6

Write the equation in slope-intercept form.

15. $-8y = 5x + 3$

16. If the change over time in the temperature T is modeled by the function $T(x) = 5x - 20$, what is the change in T per unit of time?

17. Find the x- and y-intercepts of the line $3x + 2y = 12$.

18. The cost to rent a scooter is $10 plus $8 each for each hour of use. If the cost were to be modeled with a linear equation and graphed, what would be the slope?

19. Make a scatter plot of the data and describe the correlation.

x	1	5	4	3	2	4
y	7	4	4	3	5	5

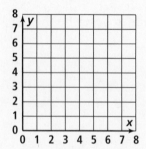

20. Graph $y = |x| - 2$ by translating $y = |x|$.

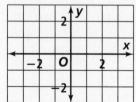

21. Use the graph to find the slope and write the equation of the line.

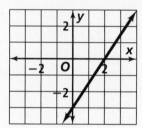

22. Are the lines $y = -\dfrac{4}{3}x + 3$ and $4x + 3y = 1$ parallel, perpendicular, or neither?

23. Is $(3, 10)$ a solution of $y \geq 5x - 8$? Explain why or why not.

24. Describe the difference between the function $f(x) = x^2$ and the function shown by the table.

x	0	1	2	3
y	1	2	5	10

25. The parents club compiled a cookbook. One company charges $750 to make a master copy and $25 for each additional copy. The total selling price depends on how many copies are ordered. Write a function rule and create a table of values to graph the rule. How much will you save per book by ordering 400 books instead of 100 books?

Quarter 3 Test

Form G

Chapters 7–9

Simplify each expression. Use positive exponents.

1. $a^{\frac{2}{3}} \cdot b^{-3}$

2. $4y^3 \cdot 7x^2 \cdot 9y^9$

3. Write 3,463,000,000 in scientific notation.

4. Write the following in order from least to greatest. 4.72×10^5, 42.7×10^2, 472, 0.0427×10^7.

5. Evaluate $y = 3 \cdot 2^x$ for $x = 1, 2,$ and 3.

6. Use a table to graph the function $y = 3 \cdot 4^x$ with domain $\{-2, -1, 0, 1, 2\}$.

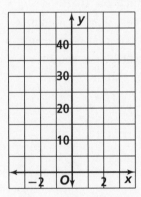

Solve each equation. If necessary, round to the nearest hundredth.

7. $4x^2 + 3 = 7x$

8. $4x^2 = 100$

9. Write an equation that models the data shown. Identify the data as *linear, quadratic,* or *exponential.*

x	1	2	3	4	5
y	3	12	27	48	75

Solve.

10. A square picture frame occupies an area of 112 ft². What is the length of each side of the picture in simplified radical form?

11. What term do you need to add to each side of $2x^2 - 8x = 9$ to complete the square?

12. What is the vertex of the equation $y = x^2 - 4x - 3$?

13. Find the number of real solutions of the equation $3x^2 - 5x + 4 = 0$.

Quarter 3 Test (continued)   *Form G*

Chapters 7–9

Simplify. Write the answer in standard form.

14. $(5x^4 - 3x^3 + 6x) + (3x^3 - 11x^2 - 8x)$

Simplify the product. Write in standard form.

15. $3x(4x^4 - 5x)$

16. Write the equation in standard form of a parabola with zeros at $x = -6$ and $x = 5$. Find the y-intercept of the parabola.

17. Factor the right side of the equation to find the zeros of the equation.
$v = x^2 + 5x - 6$

18. It takes an underwater vehicle 2 minutes to examine a square section of the seabed for every 5 m^2 of the area. Write a formula for the time T in minutes required to survey a square section of the sea floor with sides that are s meters long.

19. Write an exponential function to model the data in the following table.

x	0	1	2	3	4
y	2	6	18	54	162

20. An economist models the price of wheat with the function $P(x) = 0.15(x - 4)^2 + 2$, where x is time in months. After how many months will wheat reach its lowest price?

21. Graph the function $y = -x^2 - 2x + 1$.

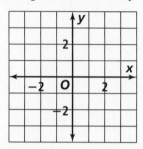

22. A construction worker drops a tool from the top of a building that is 300 feet high. The height of the tool above ground can be modeled by $h = -16t^2 + 300$, where h is height in feet and t is time in seconds.
   a. Use a table to graph this function.
   b. Use your graph to estimate the amount of time it takes for the tool to hit the ground. Round to the nearest tenth of a second.

23. The equation $y = a \cdot b^x$ models both exponential growth and exponential decay. If $a > 0$, describe the requirements for b for exponential growth, and describe the requirements for b for exponential decay.

24. Solve the system of equations.
$$y = x^2 - 6x - 8$$
$$y + 7x = 4$$

25. What effect would replacing x with $-x$ have on the graph of the function $y = x^2 - 4$?

Quarter 4 Test   *Form G*

Chapters 10–12

1. Looking at the spinner, which is the probability of spinning a number divisible by 4?

2. You remember recording bowling scores of 116, 105, 109, and 113; however, you cannot remember your score in the fifth game. You know your bowling average is 109, what did you score the fifth game?

3. Graph $y = \sqrt{x} - 4$.

4. Data Set 2 is obtained by adding 6 to each element of Data Set 1. Compare the means and ranges of the two sets.

Set 1	5	12	11	3	8
Set 2	11	18	17	9	14

5. The time for a team to finish a project varies inversely with the number of people on the team. If a project would take 2 people 6 hours to complete, write a formula for the time $T(x)$ for a team of x people to finish the work.

6. The table shows hours spent outdoors by 100 people. Find the percent probability that one of the people spent at least

4 hours outside and is at least 16 years old.

Hours Age	Less than 2	At least 2, less than 4	At least 4, less than 6	At least 6, less than 8	8 or more
6–10	2	7	8	11	15
11–15	3	2	1	3	8
16–20	6	4	2	3	5
21–25	8	2	3	2	5

7. Is the variation between P and V direct or inverse? Explain your reasoning.

V	11	22	33	44
P	0.5	1.0	1.5	2.0

8. Find the minimum, first quartile, median, third quartile, and maximum of the data set.
65 97 76 88 73 84 92 79 80 85 70 68

9. Would the histogram made from the following data appear *uniform, symmetric,* or *skewed*?
0 5 15 26 12 0 2 0 15 16 8 10 12 4

10. Based on the following histogram, how many students aged 18 to 37 graduated?

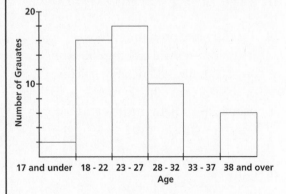

Quarter 4 Test (continued)

Form G

Chapters 10–12

11. One leg of a right triangle is 12. The hypotenuse equals 15. What is the length of the unknown leg?

12. Simplify. $\dfrac{5}{\sqrt{11} + \sqrt{7}}$

13. Solve. $x = \sqrt{4x - 3}$

14. Identify the asymptote(s) of the function. Then graph the function, $y = \dfrac{4}{x - 3}$.

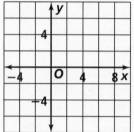

15. Writing Explain how to graph $y = \sqrt{x} + 2$ by translating the graph of $y = \sqrt{x}$.

Divide.

16. $\dfrac{x^2 - 2x - 15}{x^2} \div \dfrac{x^2 - 4x - 5}{x}$

17. $(3x^3 - 5x^2 - x + 3) \div (x - 1)$

18. This July, the probability that temperatures will rise over 80°F on any given day is 2 in 5. What is the probability that the temperature will rise over 80°F on both the first and second Sunday of the Month?

19. Solve. $\dfrac{x^2}{x - 3} = \dfrac{9}{x - 3}$

20. Find the probability that a randomly-generated number from 1 to 10 is not prime.

21. Which measure of central tendency best describes the following data set?
30 26 35 4 35 28 31

22. A landscaper chooses from 15 different shrubs for a landscape job. In how many ways can the landscaper choose 8 different shrubs? Assume the shurbs can be arranged in any order.

23. A robin flying over flat terrain sees a worm on the ground, at a sightline-distance of 140 ft. The angle of depression is 39°. How high above the ground is the robin?

24. A bag contains red and green balls. Decide whether the probabilities are of dependent or independent events.
a. A red ball is drawn, then a green ball, if the ball drawn first is replaced before the second draw
b. Two green balls are drawn in a row, if the ball drawn first is not replaced before the second draw

25. For triangle *LMN*, write the equations for sin *L* and for tan *M*.

Mid-Course Test   *Form G*

Chapters 1–6

1. At sea level, the atmosphere exerts a pressure of 450 pounds on a surface with an area of 30 square inches. How much pressure per square inch does the atmosphere exert on surfaces at sea level? Include correct units in your answer.

2. Micaela measures her floor and records its width as 3.2 m and its length as 3.8 m. She rounds her measurements to the nearest meter and estimates that the floor space in her room is 12 square meters. What is the percent error of her estimate? Round your answer to the nearest tenth of a percent.

3. The formula for simple interest is $I = prt$, where I is interest earned, p is the principal invested, r is the interest rate, and t is time. Rearrange the quantities in this formula to give a new formula for the time t.

4. Solve the proportion. $\dfrac{16}{9} = \dfrac{42}{x}$

5. The ratio of the number of right-handed students in school to the number of left-handed students in school is 9 : 1. There are 360 right-handed students in school. How many left-handed students are in school?

6. The formula for the volume of a cylinder is $V = \pi r^2 h$, where V is the volume, r is the radius of the circular base, and h is the height of the cylinder. If the radius is doubled, what will be the change in the volume of the cylinder?

7. $f(x) = x^2 + 4x + 3$. Find $f(-5)$.

Solve each equation or inequality.

8. $3x + 9 = 24$

9. $8(x - 5) = -40$

10. $-\dfrac{5}{6}y - 5 \geq 30$

11. $-5 < 2d - 1 < 3$

12. Graph the real number solutions of $2x + 4 \geq 16$.

13. Graph the solutions of the inequality $y > 2x + 3$.

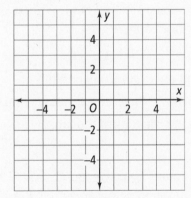

14. Write a function rule to describe the amount of change $c(x)$ from a $20 bill if you buy x pounds of grapes at $1.29 per pound.

15. What is the range of $y = x^2 - 5$ when the domain is $\{-1, 0, 3.5\}$?

Mid-Course Test (continued)   *Form G*

Chapters 1–6

16. Find the sixth term in the sequence
8, −2, −12, −22, ...

17. Is (6, 3) a solution of $2y − 9 \geq 4(x − 8)$?
Explain why or why not.

18. Tell whether the following system has
one solution, infinitely many solutions, or
no solution.

$$\frac{x}{4} + \frac{y}{9} = 27$$

$$\frac{3x}{2} + \frac{2y}{3} = 19$$

**Write an equation or inequality to model
each situation. Then solve.**

19. Mike withdrew $32 from his bank
account at an ATM. The transaction slip
said his balance was $289.14. What was
his previous balance?

20. After you put 8 gallons of gas into an
empty tank, the gas gauge reads $\frac{2}{3}$ full.
What is the capacity of the tank?

21. The perimeter for the rectangle and
regular hexagon below are equal. Find *x*.

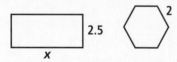

22. Fair tickets for 2 adults and 3 children
cost $34. An adult ticket costs $2 more
than a child ticket. What is the price of
an adult ticket?

23. What is the greatest number of $0.25
gumballs you can buy with $2.20?

Solve.

24. 12 is what percent of 37.5?

25. 82% of 350 is what number?

26. A package delivery company handles
14 million packages per year in the
Midwest. If this represents only 35%
of their total business how many total
packages do they handle in a year?

**Find the slope of the line passing through
each pair of points.**

27. (−3, 4) and (6, 1)

28. (4, 16) and (0, 8)

**Write the equation of the line for each of
the following conditions.**

29. through two points (2, 4) and (4, 7)

30. a horizontal line passing through the
point (6, 18)

31. parallel to the line $y = \frac{4}{9}x + 5$ through
point (−2, 1)

32. Write the equation of direct variation
that includes the point (−6, 2).

Mid-Course Test (continued)

Form G

Chapters 1–6

33. Which function has the greater value when x = 4: $y = x^3$ or the function represented by the table of values?

x	0	1	2	3
y	1	3	9	27

34. A line of best fit for a data set had the correlation coefficient $r = 0.92659$. Is this an example of positive correlation, negative correlation, or no correlation? Is this an example of a strong or weak correlation?

35. Graph the function $y = |x| - 4$ by translating $y = |x|$.

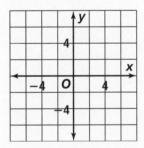

36. Write an equation representing $y = |x|$, translated 6 units to the left.

37. Using the formula $C = \dfrac{5}{9}(F - 32)$, find the Fahrenheit temperature when the Celsius temperature is 45°.

38. Mr. Smith expects to pay $19,400 in taxes. This is no more than $\dfrac{1}{3}$ of his salary. What is his least possible earned income?

39. Which property is illustrated?
$6(12 - 3) = 6(12) - 6(3)$

40. Which employee has the highest hourly rate? Keep in mind that they do not get paid for lunch.

	Total Hours Worked	Lunch Hour	Pay Before Taxes
Scott	42.5	3.5	$645.60
Mike	38.75	2.75	$629.70
Todd	40.5	3.25	$641.25
Jason	41.25	4.0	$647.50

41. Solve the following system.
$3x + 2y = 18$
$y = -\dfrac{2}{3}x + 12$

42. A person's cumulative fundraising total is shown after each week. Write a recursive rule to represent the totals as an arithmetic sequence.

1	2	3	4
$50	$80	$100	$140

Mid-Course Test (continued)   *Form G*

Chapters 1–6

43. Luis leaves home riding his bike. The graph below relates two quantities—distance from home and time in minutes—of Luis's trip.
Use the graph to write your own summary of Luis's trip. Be sure to include descriptions of Luis's relative speed during different intervals of the trip, as modeled by the graph.

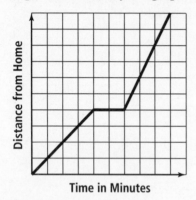

Time in Minutes

44. What is the solution of $|-2x + 5| < 60$?

45. Joe's salary in 2001 was $32,600. In 2002 he received a raise of $1560. Assume he receives the same raise every year.
  a. Write a function rule for finding Joe's salary after 2001.
  b. Find Joe's salary in 2007.

46. A boy 4 ft tall casts a shadow 6 ft long. He stands next to a monument that has a 52 ft long shadow. How tall is the monument?

47. You start a pet-sitting service. You spend $35 on advertising. You plan to charge $5 a day to watch each pet.
  a. Write an equation to relate your daily income y to the number of pets x you watch.

b. Graph the equation. What are the x- and y-intercepts?

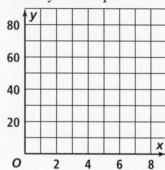

c. How many days do you need to watch a pet to pay for advertising?

48. Write a function rule for the data in the scatter plot.

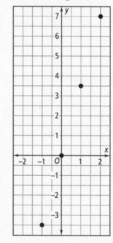

49. Suppose you receive a digital file of an image that is 25% larger than the original image. By what percent decrease would you need to reduce the image to return it to its original size?

50. Describe how you can tell whether two lines are parallel, perpendicular, or neither without graphing them.

Final Test

Form G

Chapters 1–12

1. The altitude of one airplane is given by $A_1 = 6{,}000 + 500t$, and the altitude of a second plane is given by $A_2 = 12{,}500 - 600t$. Write an equation modeling A, the difference in their altitudes.

2. Write the equation shown in the graph.

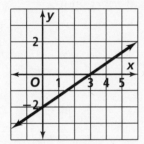

3. Gina has an meeting in 45 min. She is driving at a rate of 30 mi/h. If she is 24 mi away, will she arrive on time? If not, how early or late will she be?

4. The library fine for an overdue DVD is $2 for the first day plus $0.25 for each additional day. How many days overdue is a DVD if the fine is $3.25?

5. A 10-foot ladder leans against a wall with its foot braced 3 feet from the wall's base. How far up the wall does the ladder reach? Round to the nearest hundredth.

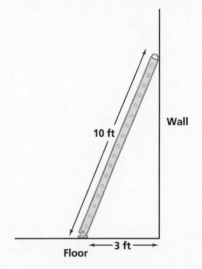

6. In 9 minutes, an athlete can run 2 kilometers. Express the athlete's average speed in meters per second. Round to the nearest tenth.

7. Simplify.
   $(6x^3 + 2x^2 - 5x) - (x^3 - 9x^2 + 4)$

Solve.

8. $4x - 11 = 7$

9. $\dfrac{8}{x + 3} = \dfrac{1}{x} + 1$

10. $\sqrt{7x - 1} = \sqrt{5x + 3}$

Final Test (continued)

Form G

Chapters 1–12

11. Graph the function $y = |x-4|$.

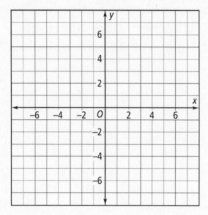

12. Solve. $6x^2 + 7x - 20 = 0$

Write in standard form the equation of a line that satisfies the given conditions.

13. perpendicular to $9x + 3y = 36$, through $(1, 2)$

14. x-intercept = 5 and y-intercept = -4

Evaluate.

15. $f(3)$ when $f(x) = 4x - 7$

16. $f(3)$ when $f(x) = 2^x - 1$

Factor.

17. $x^2 + 6x - 27$

18. $2x^3 + x^2 - 14x - 7$

19. Find the number of real number solutions of $4x^2 + 16x + 15 = 0$.

20. Find the 6th term in the sequence $-5, -9, -13, -17, \ldots$.

Simplify each radical expression.

21. $\sqrt{75} + \sqrt{3}$

22. $\sqrt{75x^2} \cdot \sqrt{3x^3}$

Simplify each expression.

23. What is the probability that, for two rolls of a number cube, the first number is 3 and the second number is higher than 3?

24. $7x^2y^{-1}(2xy^2)^3$

25. $\dfrac{4x^2y^5}{12x^3y^2z^{-3}}$

26. What is the probability of rolling a number divisible by 2 on a number cube?

Final Test (continued)   Form G

Chapters 1–12

27. One hundred college students were surveyed for their year (Freshman, Sophomore, Junior, or Senior) and the average number of hours of each week spent in extracurricular activities. The data is presented in the following table. Estimate the probability that a student in his or her first two years spends less than 6 hours each week in extracurricular activities.

Hours Year	Less than 2	At least 2, less than 4	At least 4, less than 6	At least 6, less than 8	8 or more
Freshman	12	9	2	0	2
Sophomore	4	5	9	5	2
Junior	5	1	5	8	6
Senior	10	7	4	3	1

28. Solve and graph the inequality.
$$-3 \leq -(x + 9)$$

⟵ + + + + + + + + ⟶

Find the product. Write the answer in standard form.

29. $(x^2 + 4)(x + 3)$

30. Two economists predict that the price of figs will rise over the course of the next year. The first economist uses the linear model $P(t) = 20 + \dfrac{20t}{7}$, where t is time in months. The second economist predicts that, from its starting price of 20 dollars per pound, the price will increase by 10% each month. After how many months does the second economist predict higher prices than the first economist? Round to the nearest month.

31. In a crash safety test, engineers accelerate two cars toward each other so that the distance in meters between them is modeled by $D(t) = 25 - t^2$, where t is time in seconds. What is the domain on which the model is applicable?

32. Write 375,000 in scientific notation.

33. Write an inequality describing the graph.

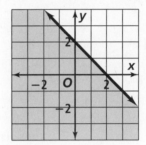

Solve each system using any method.

34. $7x + 15y = 32$
   $x = 3y + 20$

35. $y = x - 1$
   $y = -x^2 + 1$

36. Write a system of equations to model this situation. Then use your system to solve. At a garage sale a CD costs three times as much as a book. You bought three books and two CDs. You spent $18. What is the price of a CD and the price of a book?

Solve.

37. 88 is 22% of what number?

Final Test (continued)   *Form G*

Chapters 1–12

38. Jennifer is planning to buy a car. The car costs $14,500. She lives in Iowa where the sales tax is 7.2%. What is the total cost for the car?

39. The students in the band are selling entertainment books. They earn $11.25 on each book they sell. Their goal is to earn more than $7000. What is the fewest number they can sell and still reach their goal?

40. Describe the effect on the graph of the function $f(x) = 2x^2 - 6$ of replacing x with $(x+5)$ and the constant −6 with −1.

Write an equation or inequality. Then solve.

41. The sum of three consecutive integers is 219. Find the integers.

42. The Local Phone Company charges a monthly fee of $26.99 plus $0.07 for each minute of long distance up to 2000 minutes. Find the maximum and minimum number of minutes of long distance charges for customers whose monthly charge is at least $53.24 but no more than $132.00.

43. The sides of a triangular garden are 10 ft, 22 ft, and 18 ft. Is the garden in the shape of a right triangle? Justify your answer.

44. Multiply. $\dfrac{x + 2}{3x + 3} \cdot \dfrac{6x^2 - 6}{x^2 + 5x + 6}$

45. Divide.
$(4x^4 - 9x^3 - 11 + x + 2x^2 + 6x^5)$
$\div (2x^2 - 3)$

46. Suppose y varies directly with x. Write an equation for the direct variation if $y = 8$ when $x = 15$.

47. Suppose y varies inversely with x. Write an equation for the inverse variation if $y = 8$ when $x = 15$.

48. The equation for the gravitational force between two objects is given below. Solve the equation for r.

$$F_g = G\frac{m_1 m_2}{r^2}$$

49. An engineer models the changing storage capacity in amp hours of a rechargeable battery with the exponential model $A(n) = 150 \cdot 0.9975^n$, where n is the number of times the battery has been recharged. What percent of its maximum capacity does the battery lose each time it is recharged?

50. Use a table to graph the function $y = 2x^2 - 5$. Estimate the value of the x-intercepts.

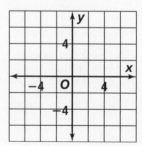

Quarter 1 Test

Form K

Chapters 1–3

Write an expression for the phrase. Use *n* to represent the unknown quantity.

1. With the return of the $2 deposit, the total rental fee came to $2 less than 3 times the hourly rate.

2. Write an explicit formula for the sequence given by the recursive definition $A(1) = 2$, and $A(n+1) = A(n) + 2$.

3. A paper glider is launched horizontally from a height of 20 feet. While in flight, its height above the ground in feet is given by the function $h(t) = -2t + 20$, where *t* is time in seconds. What is the domain of $h(t)$?

4. Name the first three numbers in the sequence.

   ___ ___ ___ 55 70 85 100 115....

5. What is the domain of the function $\{(2,10), (3,12), (4,14)\}$?

6. Solve: $\dfrac{n}{2} = \dfrac{3}{7}$

7. You have a coupon for 10% off of a lamp that costs $60. What is the discounted price of the lamp?

8. Use an equation to model the relationship shown in the table.

Day	Height
1	2 in.
2	4 in.
3	6 in.
4	8 in.

9. For $f(x) = \sqrt{x}$, estimate $f(17)$ to the nearest integer.

10. Which property is illustrated?
    $(4 \cdot 8) \cdot 6 = 4 \cdot (8 \cdot 6)$

Solve each inequality. Check your answer.

11. $x - 7 < 35$

12. $-60 \le 6x$

13. The formula for finding the area of a rectangle is $A = lw$.
    A rectangle has length 10 in. and area 20 in.^{2}. How wide is the rectangle?

Quarter 1 Test (continued)   Form K

Chapters 1–3

14. The following graph shows the distance over time between a car and a police officer. For how many seconds was the car within 150 feet or less of the officer?

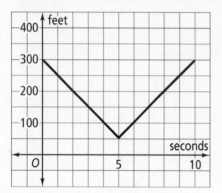

15. Which property is illustrated?
$4(5 - 2) = 4 \cdot 5 - 4 \cdot 2$

16. Write an equation to model this situation, and then use your equation to solve it.

A teacher has 72 pencils to hand out to 24 students. How many pencils does each student receive?

17. Is the sum $\dfrac{1}{4} + \dfrac{1}{2}$ a rational number?

18. Use the graph to find the solution of $f(x) = 2$.

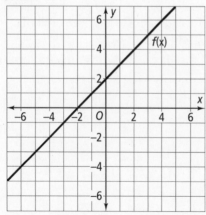

19. There are 15 dogs at a park. Ten of the dogs are small. Five of the dogs are large and have short tails. In all, eight dogs have short tails. How many dogs are small and have long tails?

Solve each equation. Check your answer.

20. $9w - 5 = 22$

21. $2(t + 4) = 10$

22. $2x + 2 = 3 + x$

23. Simplify the expression. Assume variables are not equal to zero.
$$\dfrac{20x^2y}{3x^2y^9}$$

24. How many miles will you travel in 2 h at 15 mi/h?

25. $\triangle CAB$ is similar to $\triangle EFD$. What is the length of $\overline{DE}$?

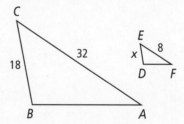

Quarter 2 Test

Chapters 4–6

Form K

Solve each system by graphing.

1. $\begin{cases} y = x + 1 \\ y = -x + 3 \end{cases}$

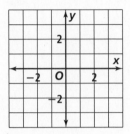

2. $\begin{cases} y < 2x - 1 \\ y \geq -x + 2 \end{cases}$

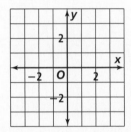

3. Solve the system using elimination.

$x + 3y = 13$

$3x - y = -11$

Write a system of equations to model each situation. Solve by any method.

4. You and some friends buy hamburgers and milkshakes for lunch. A hamburger costs $1.50 and a milkshake costs $2.00. The total bill for 12 items is $21.50. How many hamburgers and how many milkshakes did your group buy?

5. A collection of dimes and nickels is worth $0.55. There are 7 coins in all. How many dimes and how many nickels are there?

6. Suppose you plant a tree in fertile soil and provide the proper amount of water and fertilizer. The tree is healthy and grows steadily.

Sketch a graph showing what the height of the tree might look like over time.

7. Model the rule $f(x) = -2x + 1$ with a table and a graph.

8. The table shows a hospital's patient count for two successive days. Write a linear function using the data (with x representing the day number), and then use the model to predict the patient count on Day 3.

Day 1	295
Day 2	272

9. Write an equation in point-slope form for the line through the point $(1, -4)$ with slope $m = -3$.

10. What is the range of $f(x) = 3x - 5$ when the domain is $\{-6, 4, 8\}$?

Write a function rule to describe the statement.

11. the amount of medicine $m(x)$ left in an 8 oz bottle after x doses of 0.25 oz each

12. Write the equation of direct variation that includes the point $(4, -8)$.

Find the common difference in each arithmetic sequence. Then find the next two terms.

13. $-7, -4, -1, 2, \ldots$

14. $21, 33, 45, 57, \ldots$

Write the equation in slope-intercept form.

15. $2y = 4x + 6$

Quarter 2 Test (continued)

Form K

Chapters 4–6

16. If the balance in a checking account B is modeled by the function $B(x) = -x + 1500$, what is the change in B per unit of time?

17. Find the x- and y-intercepts of the line $x + y = 3$.

18. The cost to hire movers is $200 plus $50 each for each hour they work. If the cost were to be modeled with a linear equation, what would be the slope?

19. Make a scatter plot of the data and describe the correlation.

x	2	6	5	4	3	5
y	7	4	4	3	5	5

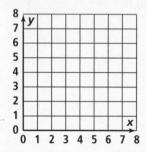

20. Graph $y = |x + 2|$ by translating $y = |x|$.

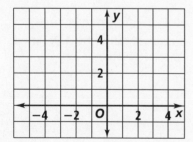

21. Use the graph to find the slope and write the equation of the line.

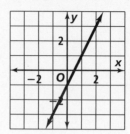

22. Are the lines $y = -\frac{1}{2}x$ and $y = 2x$ parallel, perpendicular, or neither?

23. Determine whether $(2, 8)$ is a solution of $y \geq 2x + 3$. Explain why or why not.

24. Compare the slope of the function $f(x) = 2x + 1$ to the slope of the function shown by the table.

x	0	1	2	3
y	0	2	4	6

25. A high school has designed its yearbook. A company charges $900 to assemble the master copy and $42 to make each additional copies. The total selling price depends on how many copies are made. Write a function rule and make a table of values to construct a graph. How much will the school save on each book by ordering 600 instead of 200?

Quarter 3 Test

Form K

Chapters 7–9

Simplify each expression. Use positive exponents.

1. $\dfrac{x^3y^{-1}}{y}$

2. $2x^3 \cdot 3x^2 \cdot 2y$

3. Write 7,402,000 in scientific notation.

4. Write the following in order from least to greatest. 23.6×10^3, 2.36×10^2, 2.36×10^3

5. Evaluate $y = 3 \cdot 2^x$ for $x = 0$, 1, and 2.

6. Use a table to graph the function $y = \dfrac{1}{2} \cdot (2^x)$ with domain $\{-2, -1, 0, 1, 2\}$.

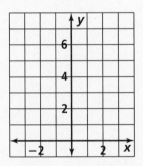

Solve each equation. If necessary, round your answer to the nearest hundredth.

7. $x^2 - 8x = -12$

8. $x^2 = 16$

9. Write an equation that models the data shown. Identify the data as *linear*, *quadratic*, or *exponential*.

x	-1	0	1	2	3
y	0.5	1	2	4	8

Solve.

10. A square garden has an area of 75 ft². What is the length of each side of the plot in simplified radical form?

11. What term do you need to add to each side of $x^2 + 6x = -15$ to complete the square?

12. What is the vertex of the equation $y = x^2 - 6x + 4$?

13. Find the number of real solutions of the equation $y = 5x^2 + 10x + 3$.

Simplify. Write the answer in standard form.

14. $(x^2 - 4x + 5) - (3x^2 + 7x + 3)$

Simplify the product. Write in standard form.

15. $4x(6x^3 - 10x)$

16. Write the equation in standard form of the upward-opening parabola with zeros at x equal to –6 and –4. Also find the y-intercept of the parabola.

Quarter 3 Test (continued)   Form K

Chapters 7–9

17. Factor the right side of the equation to find the zeros of the equation.
$y = x^2 + 12x + 11$

18. The time it takes for an art archivist to clean and restore a square section of a Renaissance painting is 20 minutes for every square centimeter of the area. Write a formula for the amount of time T in minutes required to clean and restore a square oil painting with sides that are s centimeters long.

19. Write an explicit function to model the data in the following table.

x	0	1	2	3	4
y	3	30	300	3000	30,000

20. An economist predicts that the price in dollars of an ounce of gold will change according to the function $P(x) = 20 \cdot (x - 6)^2 + 1500$, where x is time in months. After how many months does the economist predict gold to reach its lowest price?

21. Graph the function $y = 3x^2 - 2$.

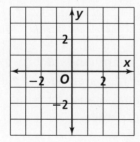

22. A stone falls from a cliff that is 500 feet high. The height of the stone above ground can be modeled by $h = -16t^2 + 500$, where h is height in feet and t is time in seconds.

   a. Use a table to graph this function.

   b. Use your graph to estimate the amount of time it takes for the stone to hit the ground. Round your answer to the nearest tenth of a second.

23. Does the equation $y = a \cdot b^x$ model exponential growth or exponential decay when $a > 0$ and $0 < b < 1$?

24. Solve the system of equations.
$y = x^2$
$y = -3x - 2$

25. What effect would replacing x with $x + 2$ have on the graph of the function $f(x) = x^2$?

Quarter 4 Test

Chapters 10–12

Form K

1. Refer to the spinner below. What is the probability of landing on a green space?

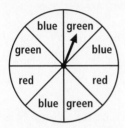

2. Your average is 86 after taking three tests. Two of your scores were 88 and 83. What was your score on the third test?

3. Graph $y = \sqrt{x} - 3$.

4. Data Set 2 is obtained by adding 2 to each element of Data Set 1. Compare the means and ranges of the two sets.

Set 1	8	3	10	3	4
Set 2	10	5	12	5	6

5. The time for the council to make a decision varies directly with the number of council members present. If it takes 6 hours for 4 members to decide, write a formula for the time $T(x)$ for x members to make a decision.

6. The table below shows the numbers of full- and part-time workers at 50 companies. Find the probability that a company has more than 10 full-time and no more than 10 part-time workers.

Full-time / Part-time	0–5	6–10	11–15	16–20
0–5	2	1	6	1
6–10	0	3	5	2
11–15	2	3	8	17

7. Based on the data, is there a *direct variation* or an *inverse variation*? Explain your reasoning.

Volunteers	5	10	20
Hours	12	6	3

8. Find the minimum, first quartile, median, third quartile, and maximum of the data set.
   70 73 79 80 84 85 92

9. Would a histogram of the data below appear *uniform, symmetric,* or *skewed*?
   0 0 0 1 4 5 5 7 7 9 9 15

10. According to the following histogram, how many subway riders spent 6 or more hours riding the subway?

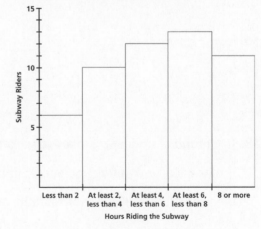

Quarter 4 Test (continued)   *Form K*

Chapters 10–12

11. The legs of a right triangle are 3 and 4. What is the hypotenuse?

12. Simplify. $\dfrac{1}{\sqrt{5} + \sqrt{3}}$

13. Solve. $x = \sqrt{7x - 6}$

14. Identify the asymptote(s) of the function. Then graph the function $y = \dfrac{2}{x - 1} + 3$.

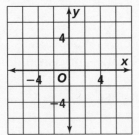

15. Writing Explain how to graph $y = \sqrt{x} - 3$ by translating the graph of $y = \sqrt{x}$.

Divide.

16. $\dfrac{x}{8 - 2x} \div \dfrac{2x}{4 - x}$

17. $(x^3 + 4x^2 + 8x + 5) \div (x + 1)$

18. In a group of students, $\dfrac{1}{3}$ take French and $\dfrac{4}{9}$ of them take Computer Science. Find the probability that a random student from the group is taking both courses.

19. Solve $\dfrac{x^2}{x - 2} = \dfrac{4}{x - 2}$.

20. What is the probability that a randomly-generated integer from 1 to 10 is a multiple of 3 or 4?

21. Which measure of central tendency best describes the following data set?
Yes Yes No Maybe No Maybe Yes Yes

22. Six students are trying out for 2 different roles in a school play. In how many ways can the 2 roles be filled?

23. The string of a kite is 100 ft long and is held against a flat area of ground. It makes an angle of 40° with the ground. How high is the kite? Round to the nearest tenth.

24. Decide whether the probabilities are of dependent or independent events.
a. From a box containing doughnuts of 3 types, two people choosing a doughnut at random get the same type
b. The star players of two teams both miss the same game due to injuries

25. Find sin A and tan B of triangle ABC.

Mid-Course Test

Form K

Chapters 1–6

Simplify each expression.

1. In Bill's part-time job he used the company vehicle and traveled 30 miles in 45 minutes. What was his average speed in miles per hour?

2. John measures the patio in his yard and records its width as 4.1 m and its length as 4.9 m. He rounds his measurements to the nearest meter and estimates that the patio in his yard is about 20 square meters. What is the percent error of his estimate? Round your answer to the nearest tenth of a percent.

3. The formula for the area of a rectangle is $A = bh$, where A is the area, b is the base, and h is the height. Rearrange the quantities in this formula to give a new formula for the height h

4. Solve the proportion. $\dfrac{x}{3} = \dfrac{12}{9}$

5. A pet store has 3 dogs for every 2 cats. If there are 15 dogs at the store, how many cats are there?

6. The formula for the area of a circle is $A = \pi r^2$, where r is the radius of the circle. If the radius is tripled, what will be the change in the area of the circle?

7. $f(x) = x^2 + 2x + 1$. Find $f(4)$.

Solve each equation or inequality. Then check.

8. $3x + 1 = 13$

9. $2(y + 1) = 6$

10. $3y + 2 > 8$

11. $2 < x + 1 < 5$

Solve and graph each inequality.

12. $4x - 5 < 19$

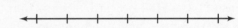

13. Graph the solutions of the inequality $y < -2x$.

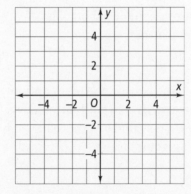

14. Write a function rule to describe the cost of x pounds of apples that cost $1.39 per pound.

15. What is the range of $y = 2x^2$ when the domain is $\{0,1,2\}$?

Mid-Course Test (continued)

Form K

Chapters 1–6

16. Find the next two terms in the arithmetic sequence. 76, 89, 102, 115, . . .

17. Is (6, 3) a solution of $2y \geq x - 8$? Explain why or why not.

18. Tell whether the following system has *one solution, infinitely many solutions,* or *no solution.*

$x + y = 8$
$2x + 2y = 16$

Solve each problem.

19. Jason has a $100 gift card. After he makes a $39 purchase, how much money remains on the gift card?

20. You can fill the gas tank of a lawn mower 4 times from a single gallon of gas. What is the capacity of the gas tank?

21. Tickets to the zoo for one adult and two children cost $17. An adult ticket costs $2 more than a child's ticket. What is the price of an adult ticket?

22. Write and simplify an equation for the perimeter *P* of the figure shown. If the perimeter is 22, find *x*.

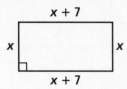

23. Write an inequality to find *T* the greatest number of $0.50 tickets you can buy with *x* dollars.

Write an equation to model each question and solve.

24. What is 25% of 80?

25. 85% of 300 is what number?

26. In a survey 650 out of 1200 people change the oil in their car every 3000 miles. What percent of the people change their oil every 3000 miles?

27. Find the slope of the line.

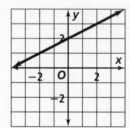

28. Find the slope of the line passing through the points (1, 4) and (3, 16).

29. Write the equation of the line passing through the points (0, 0) and (1, 2).

30. Write the equation of the vertical line passing through the point (5, 3).

Mid-Course Test (continued)   *Form K*

Chapters 1–6

31. What is the slope of a line that is parallel to the line $y = 5x + 3$?

32. Write the equation of a direct variation that includes the given point. $(3, 9)$

33. Which function has the greater value when $x = 3$: $y = x^2$ or the function represented by the table of values?

x	0	1	2
y	1	2	4

34. A line of best fit was drawn for a set of data. The correlation coefficient calculated was $r = 0.102$. Is this an example of positive correlation, negative correlation, or no correlation? Is this an example of a strong or weak correlation?

35. Graph the function $y = x - 2$, by translating $y = x$.

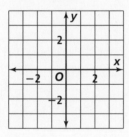

36. Does the equation $y = |x| + 3$ translate $y = |x|$ 3 units up or 3 units down? Use the point $(0, 0)$ to explain your answer.

37. What is the width of a rectangle with area 30 ft^2 and length 5 ft?

38. Tips make up no more than $\frac{1}{4}$ of Jen's income. If Jen earned \$240 in total income for one week, what was the maximum amount she received in tips?

39. Which property is illustrated?
$2(3 - 1) = 2(3) - 2(1)$

40. While shopping, you find that a 12-oz package of Brand A costs \$2.40 and a 16-oz package of Brand B costs \$2.50. Which brand has a lower unit cost?

41. Solve the following system.
$3x + y = 18$
$y = 12$

Mid-Course Test (continued)   *Form K*

Chapters 1–6

42. A person's cumulative savings account total is shown after each week. Write a recursive rule to represent the totals as an arithmetic sequence.

1	2	3	4
$20	$45	$70	$95

43. On a graph that relates distance with time, what does a horizontal line tell you about the speed of the object modeled by the graph?

44. What is the solution of $|x| + 4 < 8$?

45. Dwayne received a $50 bonus at work last month. His company announced that the bonuses would be increased by $5 each month. Write a function rule representing Dwayne's bonus plan after x months.

46. The two triangles shown are similar. What is the length of x?

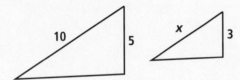

47. Suppose you advertise your babysitting services at an hourly rate of $6 plus $2 for each child.

  a. Write an equation relating your total hourly rate y to the number of children x that you watch.

  b. Graph the equation. What is the y − intercept?

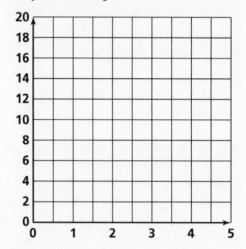

48. Write a function rule for the data in the scatter plot.

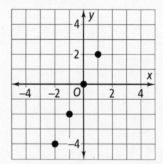

49. A plant grows from 12 inches tall to 18 inches tall. What is the percent increase in the plant's height?

50. When you multiply the slopes of two lines, you get −1. What does this tell you about the relationship between the lines?

Final Test

Form K

Chapters 1–12

1. Starting at time $t = 0$, the altitude of one helicopter is given by $A_1 = 600 + 150t$, and the altitude of a second helicopter is given by $A_2 = 1250 + 50t$. Write an equation modeling A, the difference in their altitudes.

2. What is the equation of the graph shown below?

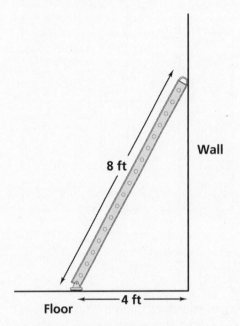

Solve each problem.

3. Jonna needs to travel 496 miles in 8 hours. How fast does she need to go in order to reach her destination on time?

4. A local Internet provider offers a plan in which you pay a flat fee of $5.95 per month plus $0.20 per hour of use. For how many hours of use were you billed if your monthly bill is $8.95?

5. If an 8-foot ladder is leaned against a wall with its foot braced 4 feet from the wall's base, how far up the wall will the top of the ladder reach? Round to the nearest hundredth.

6. In 4 minutes, an athlete can run 1 kilometer. Express the athlete's average speed in meters per second. Round to the nearest tenth.

7. $(x^2 + 3x + 4) + (2x + 4)$

Solve.

8. $2x - 4 = 10$

9. $\dfrac{6x}{x + 4} = (x - 1)$

Final Test (continued)   *Form K*

Chapters 1–12

10. $\sqrt{3x} = \sqrt{x+4}$

11. Graph the equation $y = |x+3|$.

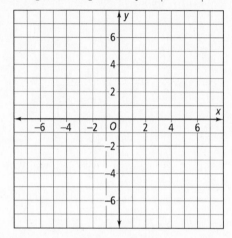

12. $x^2 + 6x + 8 = 0$

Write in standard form the equation of a line that satisfies the given conditions.

13. perpendicular to a line with slope $= -\dfrac{1}{3}$, through $(1, 1)$

14. through $(0, -3)$ and $(-4, 0)$

Evaluate.

15. $f(4)$ when $f(x) = 2x + 3$

16. $f(4)$ when $f(x) = 2x^2$

Factor.

17. $x^2 + 8x + 12$

18. $x^2 + 2x + 3x + 6$

19. Use the discriminant to find the number of real solutions of $2x^2 + 9x + 7 = 0$.

20. Find the next two terms in the arithmetic sequence. $4, 8, 12, \ldots$

Simplify each radical expression.

21. $\sqrt{8} + \sqrt{2}$

22. $\sqrt{8x^2} \cdot \sqrt{2x^2}$

23. What is the probability that, for two rolls of a number cube, the first number is odd and the second number is even?

Simplify each expression.

24. $2x^{-1}(2x^3)^2$

25. $\dfrac{6x^2y^3}{2xy^{-1}}$

26. What is the probability of rolling an odd number on a number cube?

Final Test (continued)

Form K

Chapters 1–12

27. One hundred high school students were surveyed for their year (freshman, sophomore, junior, or senior) and the average number of hours of each week spent listening to music. The data is presented in the following table. Estimate the probability that a student in his or her junior or senior year spends less than 8 hours each week listening to music.

Hours Year	Less than 4	At least 4, less than 8	At least 8, less than 12	At least 12, less than 16	16 or more
Freshman	5	4	9	3	4
Sophomore	3	5	11	5	1
Junior	4	2	8	6	5
Senior	1	6	12	2	4

28. Solve and graph the inequality.
$4x - 3 < 17$

Find the product. Write the answer in standard form.

29. $(x^2 + 1)(x + 2)$

30. Two economists predict that the price of lobster meat, in dollars per pound, will rise over the course of the next year. The first economist uses the linear model $P(t) = 10 + \frac{6}{5}t$, where t is time in months. The second economist predicts that, from its starting price of 10 dollars per pound, the price will increase by a factor of 10% each month. After how many months does the second economist predict higher prices for lobster meat than the linear model? Round to the nearest month.

31. The balance on your account with a movie rental service is $B(m) = 25 - 5m$, where m is the number of movies you rent. When $B(m) = 0$, you have to add more money to your account in order to rent more movies. What is the domain on which the model is applicable?

32. Write 45,000 in scientific notation.

33. Graph $y > \frac{1}{3}x - 2$.

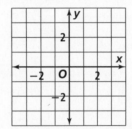

Solve each system using any method.

34. $3x - y = 13$
$2x + 3y = 16$

35. $6x - 2y = 8$
$5x - 2y = 5$

36. Write a system of equations to model this situation. Then use your system to solve it.
A parking lot has twice as many cars as trucks. The total number of cars and trucks in the parking lot is 24. How many cars and how many trucks are in the lot?

Final Test (continued)   Form K

Chapters 1–12

Solve.

37. 3 is 60% of what number?

38. Frank is planning to buy a portable music player. The player costs $30, and the sales tax is 8%. What is the total cost of the music player?

39. Joan must save at least $500 to open a savings account. She saves $80 each month toward her goal. What is the fewest number of months before Joan can open the account?

40. Describe the effect on the graph of the function $y = |x|$ of replacing x with $(x + 2)$.

Write an equation or inequality. Then solve.

41. The sum of two consecutive even numbers is 30. Find the numbers.

42. An amusement park has an entrance fee of $25 and charges an additional $2 for each ride. Find the maximum and minimum number of rides seen by a small group of visitors whose total fee is at least $37 but no more than $53.

43. Find x.

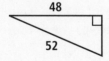

44. Multiply. $\dfrac{x + 2}{6x + 6} \cdot \dfrac{x + 1}{x^2 + 5x + 6}$

45. Divide. $(x^2 + 4x + 5) \div (x + 1)$

46. Suppose y varies directly with x. Write an equation for the direct variation if $y = 4$ when $x = 2$.

47. Suppose y varies inversely with x. Write an equation for the inverse variation if $y = 4$ when $x = 2$.

48. The equation for the area of a circle is given below. Solve the equation for r.
$A = \pi r^2$

49. A conservationist models the changing world population of an endangered species with the exponential model $A(n) = 600 \cdot 0.96^n$, where n is the number of years since 2010. What percent of its population does this species lose each year?

50. Make a table of values and graph the function $y = x^2 - 2$.

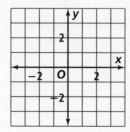

End-of-Course Assessment

Selected Response

Read each question. Then circle the letter(s) of the correct answer(s).

1. A student is 5 ft 9 in. tall. Which of the following are equivalent to the student's height? Use the fact that 1 m ≈ 3.28 ft.

   A 1.75 m

   B 17.5 cm

   C 1750 cm

   D 1750 mm

2. Which is the simplified form of the expression?

   $9(r + 3) - \frac{1}{2}(4r - 16)$

   A $11r + 19$

   B $11r + 35$

   C $7r + 19$

   D $7r + 35$

3. Which model is most appropriate for the set?

   $(2, 17), (6, 121), (0, 1), (3, 34), (-1, 2), (-7, 0)$

   A Linear

   B Exponential

   C Quadratic

   D Logarithmic

4. If $f(x) = \frac{3}{4}x + \frac{5}{6}$, what is $f(12)$?

   A $\frac{59}{6}$

   B $\frac{47}{6}$

   C $\frac{23}{6}$

   D 19

5. Which function rule is graphed below?

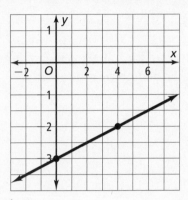

   A $y = 3x - 4$

   B $y = \frac{1}{4}x - 3$

   C $y = -\frac{1}{4}x - 3$

   D $y = \frac{1}{2}x - 3$

6. Solve $y = 2xz^2 - xy$ for x.

   A $x = \frac{1}{2z^2}$

   B $x = \frac{y}{2z^2}$

   C $x = \frac{1}{2z^2 - 1}$

   D $x = \frac{y}{2z^2 - y}$

7. Which of the following are equivalent to the polynomial?

   $4x(2x^2 - 1) + x(8x)$

   A $4x(2x^2 + 2x - 1)$

   B $8x^3 + 8x^2 - 4x$

   C $6x^3 + 8x^2 - 4x$

   D $8x^3 - 8x^2 + 4x$

8. What is the factored form of $3x^2 - 17x = 28$?

A $(x + 7)(3x - 4) = 0$

B $(x + 7)(3x + 4) = 0$

C $(x - 7)(3x - 4) = 0$

D $(x - 7)(3x + 4) = 0$

9. Which of the following give a definition for the geometric sequence?
$3, -3, 3, -3, 3, \ldots$

A $a_1 = -3; a_n = a_{n-1} \cdot -1$

B $a_n = 3 \cdot (-1)^{n-1}$

C $a_1 = 3; a_n = a_{n-1} \cdot 1$

D $a_1 = 3; a_n = a_{n-1} \cdot -1$

10. Mandy works part-time to earn money for a trip. The amount she saves after working x hours is given by the equation $y = 7.5x + 40$. How much does Mandy earn per hour?

A $7.50

B $32.50

C $40

D $47.50

11. Express the following sentence in equation form.

Five times the difference of a number and 2 is equal to the quotient of the same number and 6.

A $5x - 2 = \dfrac{x}{6}$

B $5(x - 2) = \dfrac{x}{6}$

C $5(2 - x) = \dfrac{x}{6}$

D $5(x - 2) = \dfrac{6}{x}$

12. Which of the following result in an irrational number?

A the sum of two rational numbers

B the product of two rational numbers

C the sum of a rational number and an irrational number

D the product of a nonzero rational number and an irrational number

13. The graph of which equation is shown below?

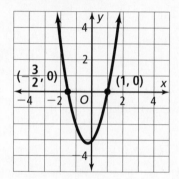

A $y = 2x^2 + x - 3$

B $y = \dfrac{1}{2}x^2 + x - 3$

C $y = 4x^2 + x - 3$

D $y = x^2 + x - 3$

14. The graph of which equation is shown below?

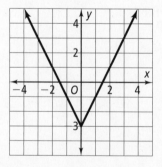

A $y = -|2x| + 3$

B $y = |2x| - 3$

C $y = |2x - 3|$

D $y = 2|x - 3|$

15. Solve the equation $2x^2 + 3x = 2$.

A -2

B $-\dfrac{1}{2}$

C $\dfrac{1}{2}$

D 2

16. Which of the following are equivalent forms of the equation $y = -\dfrac{5}{9}x + \dfrac{2}{3}$?

A $y + 1 = -\dfrac{5}{9}(x - 3)$

B $5x + 9y = 6$

C $\dfrac{5}{9}x + y = \dfrac{2}{3}$

D $-5x + 9y = 6$

17. An engineer studied the sales of trucks and SUVs in California over an 8-year period. The results are modeled in thousands sold with the following polynomials.

Trucks: $-13x^3 + 89x^2 - 119x + 6814$
SUVs: $16x^2 - 12x + 2152$

In each polynomial, $x = 0$ corresponds to the first year in the 8-year period. Which polynomial models the total number of trucks and SUVs sold in California during the 8-year period?

A $-13x^3 + 105x^2 - 131x + 8966$
B $-13x^3 + 73x^2 - 107x + 4662$
C $-13x^3 + 105x^2 - 107x + 8966$
D $13x^3 - 73x^2 + 107x - 4662$

18. At which point do the graphs of the equations intersect?

$$\begin{cases} y = 3x - 5 \\ y = |x - 7| \end{cases}$$

A $(-1, 8)$

B $(3, 4)$

C $(-1, -8)$

D $(3, -4)$

19. Which of the following correlations represents a causal relationship?

A the number of cats and the number of dogs in a shelter

B the number of cats in a shelter and the amount of cat food used

C the number of cats in a shelter and the number of vaccinations given

D the amount of money in the cash drawer and the number of cats in the shelter

20. Which of the following are solutions to the inequality $-9 \le 2x + 1 \le 5$

A -6 **D** 0

B -4 **E** 2

C -2 **F** 4

21. Which of the following are solutions to the inequality $x^2 - 4 = x + 8$

A -4

B -3

C 3

D 4

22. Which of the following are equivalent to 18 feet per minute?

    A 3.6 inches per hour

    B 40 inches per minute

    C 1080 feet per hour

    D 12,960 inches per hour

23. Which points are in the solution set for $4x - y > 1$?

    A $(1, 2)$ **D** $(2, 0)$

    B $(0, -1)$ **E** $(-1, 2)$

    C $(0, 2)$ **F** $(-1, -2)$

24. At which points do the graphs of the following equations intersect?

$$\begin{cases} y = x^2 + 9x + 1 \\ x - y = 6 \end{cases}$$

    A $(0, -6)$ **E** $(-1, -7)$

    B $(0, 1)$ **F** $(-1, 0)$

    C $(-4, -9)$ **G** $(-7, -13)$

    D $(-4, -19)$ **H** $(-7, 0)$

25. What are the factors of the expression $x^2 - 7x - 44$?

    A $(x - 11)$

    B $(x - 4)$

    C $(x + 4)$

    D $(x + 11)$

Constructed Response

In this section, show all your work in the space beneath each test item.

26. Solve the equation. Show your work and justify each step.

$$4\left(x - \frac{1}{2}\right) - 12 = 0$$

27. The perimeter of a rectangle is $6x^2 - 6x - 4$. The width of the rectangle is $2x + 1$. What is the length of the rectangle?

28. Graph the inequality $4x + 2y < 6$.

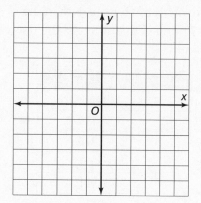

29. Graph the function $f(x) = -x^2 + 2x + 4$.

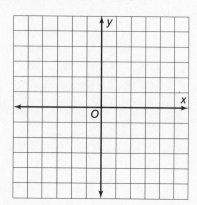

30. The ages of the members of a hiking club are 17, 18, 24, 28, 32, 36, 43, and 52. A new members who is 45 years old joins the club. In general, describe how this will affect the mean, median, mode, and range of the ages of the members of the club.

31. What are the solutions of the equation $x^2 - 4x - 32 = 0$? Show your work and justify each step.

32. One angle of an obtuse triangle measures four times the first angle. The third angle measures 30° less than the first angle. What are the degree measures of the three angles? Show or explain your work.

33. What is the solution to the system of equations?

$$\begin{cases} y = 2x + 3 \\ y = -x + 6 \end{cases}$$

34. You buy x pounds of strawberries for $3.99/lb. Write a function rule for the amount of change C you receive from a $20 bill.

35. Write an equation for the line of best fit for the scatter plot below.

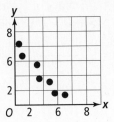

36. A square has sides measuring $5\sqrt{9}$ m. What is the area of the square?

37. Suppose you survey each coach at a cheerleading tournament. What relationship would you expect between the number of coaches and the number of teams competing in the tournament?

38. The population of a town is 75,000 and decreases 1.5% each year. If the trend continues, what will the population be after 12 years? Round your answer to the nearest thousand.

39. A beach club made $39,100 in May and $59,200 in August. What is the rate of change in the profit for this time period?

40. Write a sequence that is both arithmetic and geometric.

41. What function does the table represent?

x	−2	−1	0	1	2
y	4	5	6	7	8

42. What is the value of the function $f(x) = \dfrac{1}{3}(-5x) + 3$ when $x = 0.25$?

43. What is the correlation coefficient of the line of best fit for the data in the table? Round your answer to the nearest thousandth.

Attendance at Water Park	
Month	**Attendance**
April	130
May	276
June	874
July	951
August	712
September	402

44. A puddle is 0.06 m deep after 1 h and 0.03 m deep after 5 h. At what rate is the level of the water changing?

45. How does the graph of $y = 3x - 1$ differ from that of $y = 3x$?

46. Write an inequality for the graph below.

47. What is the solution of the system of equations?

$$\begin{cases} y = 4x - 1 \\ y = 3x + 2 \end{cases}$$

48. What is the mean of the data?
$6x, 3x, 17x, 4x, 10x, 2x$

49. What is the standard deviation of the data set rounded to the nearest thousandth?

7.2, 9.1, 5.7, 8.5, 10.2, 9.9, 11.0, 7.7, 6.4, 8.9

50. What is the vertex of the graph of the function $f(x) = x^2 + 4x - 5$?

51. What is the value of x? Explain each step in your solution.

$$\frac{1}{10}(1.2x - 3.5) = 0.13$$

52. Is the relation a function? Explain how you know.

$\{(300, 9), (260, 4), (275, 4), (350, 11),$
$(225, 2), (300, 7), (325, 10), (280, 5)\}$

53. Write an explicit formula for the arithmetic sequence.

$\dfrac{2}{3}, \dfrac{3}{4}, \dfrac{5}{6}, \dfrac{11}{12}, 1, \ldots$

54. In the following situation, is there likely to be a correlation? If so, does the situation reflect a causal relationship?

the cost per pound of salad at a salad bar and the amount of salad sold

55. In May, your savings account balance was $1140. In August, the balance in the account was $1450. What is the average rate of change per month?

Extended Response

In this section, show all your work in the space beneath each test item.

56. A ball is thrown directly upward from a height of 30 ft with an initial velocity of 64 ft/s. The equation $h = -16t^2 + 64t + 30$ gives the height h after t seconds.

   a. How long does it take for the ball to reach its maximum height? Show or explain your work.

   b. What values can be used for the domain?

57. Refer to the table below.

x	1	1.5	2	2.5	3	3.5	4
y	5	6	5	7	6.5	7.5	8

   a. Make a scatter plot of the data.

   b. Estimate an equation of the line of best fit.

58. A banquet hall charges $750 to feed large parties. For a family reunion, the cost will be divided equally among each attending family member. Each person also must pay $3.50 for a tip.

    a. Approximately how many people must attend the reunion in order for the total cost per person to be about $15 per person?

    b. Describe the change in the cost per person as the number of family members who attend the reunion increases.

59. The table shows the average weight for girls between 2 and 7 years old.

Average Weight for Girls						
Age (years)	2	3	4	5	6	7
Weight (lb)	28.4	30.8	35.2	39.6	46.2	50.6

    a. What is the slope of a trend line for the data rounded to the nearest tenth? What does the slope tell you about the situation in this problem?

    b. What is the correlation coefficient of age and weight to three decimal places? What does the correlation coefficient tell you about the situation in this problem?

60. Consider the equation $x^2 + 4x + 1$.

    a. What are the solutions to the equation?

    b. Explain why completing the square is a better strategy for solving this equation than graphing or factoring.

61. A farmer records his profits for the week from selling corn at the farmers market.

Corn Profits				
Corn sold (lb)	22	31	66	73
Profit ($)	132	186	396	438

    a. Do the values in the table represent a function? Explain how you know.

    b. How much profit does the farmer make for each pound of corn? How many pounds of corn would the farmer need to sell to earn a profit of $540?

62. A student found the solutions of $0 = x^2 - 5x - 24$ to be $x = 3$ and $x = -8$.

    a. Is the student correct? If not, what are the solutions of the equation?

    b. Graph the equation $y = x^2 - 5x - 24$ on the grid below.

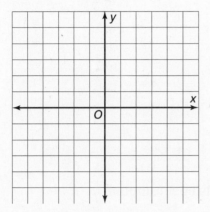

63. A cell phone plan costs \$35 per month plus 5 cents for each minute of use.

    a. Write a function for the cost of the plan. What are the domain and range of the function?

    b. How much would you expect your monthly bill to be if you used 345.6 minutes last month?

64. The surface area of a cylinder is given by the equation $2\pi r^2 + 2\pi rh$, where r is the radius of the cylinder and h is the height of the cylinder.

  a. What is the surface area of a cylinder with radius $x - 1$ and height $2x$?

  b. Find the surface area of the cylinder from part (a) if $x = 11$.

65. Consider this system of equations.

$$\begin{cases} 7x + 2y = 16 \\ -21x - 6y = 24 \end{cases}$$

  a. Find the solution of the system of equations using substitution.

  b. Solve both equations for y. What can you say about the graphs of these equations?

End-of-Course Assessment Report

CCSS Standards	Test Item(s)	Type	Algebra 1 Student Edition Lesson(s)
Use properties of rational and irrational numbers			
N.RN.B.3 Explain why the sum or product of two rational numbers is rational; that the sum of a rational number and an irrational number is irrational; and that the product of a nonzero rational number and an irrational number is irrational.	12	SR	1–6
Reason quantitatively and use units to solve problems			
N.Q.A.1 Use units as a way to understand problems and to guide the solution of multi-step problems; choose and interpret units consistently in formulas; choose and interpret the scale and the origin in graphs and data displays.	1 22	SR SR	2–6 2–6
Interpret the structure of expressions			
A.SSE.A.1 Interpret expressions that represent a quantity in terms of its context.	34 64B	CR ER	4–5 1–2
A.SSE.A.1.a Interpret parts of an expression, such as terms, factors, and coefficients.	10 25	SR SR	4–5 8–5
A.SSE.A.2 Use the structure of an expression to identify ways to rewrite it.	2	SR	1–7
Write expressions in equivalent forms to solve problems			
A.SSE.B.3.a Choose and produce an equivalent form of an expression to reveal and explain properties of the quantity represented by the expression. Factor a quadratic expression to reveal the zeros of the function it defines.	8	SR	9–4
Perform arithmetic operations on polynomials			
A.APR.A.1 Understand that polynomials form a system analogous to the integers; namely, they are closed under the operations of addition, subtraction, and multiplication; add, subtract, and multiply polynomials.	7 17 27 64A	SR SR CR ER	8–2 8–1 8–1 8–1
Understand the relationship between zeros and factors of polynomial			
A.APR.B.3 Identify zeros of polynomials when suitable factorizations are available, and use the zeros to construct a rough graph of the function defined by the polynomial.	62A	ER	9–3
Create equations that describe numbers or relationships			
A.CED.A.1 Create equations and inequalities in one variable and use them to solve problems.	11 32 36 58A	SR CR CR ER	4–5 2–3 10–2 4–6
A.CED.A.2 Create equations in two or more variables to represent relationships between quantities; graph equations on coordinate axes with labels and scales.	41	CR	5–4
A.CED.A.4 Rearrange formulas to highlight a quantity of interest, using the same reasoning as in solving equations.	6 16 65B	SR SR ER	2–5 2–5 5–6

CCSS Standards	Test Item(s)	Type	Algebra 1 Student Edition Lesson(s)
Understand solving equations as a process of reasoning and explain the reasoning			
A.REI.A.1 Explain each step in solving a simple equation as following from the equality of numbers asserted at the previous step, starting from the assumption that the original equation has a solution. Construct a viable argument to justify a solution method.	26 51 60B	CR CR ER	2–3 2–3 9–5
Solve equations and Inequalities in one variable			
A.REI.B.3 Solve linear equations and inequalities in one variable, including equations with coefficients represented by letters.	20	SR	3–6
A.REI.B.4.a Solve quadratic equations in one variable. Use the method of completing the square to transform any quadratic equation in x into an equation of the form $(x - p)^2 = q$ that has the same solutions. Derive the quadratic formula from this form.	21 31 60A	SR CR ER	9–4 9–5 9–5
A.REI.B.4.b Solve quadratic equations in one variable. Solve quadratic equations by inspection (e.g. for $x^2 = 49$), taking square roots, completing the square, the quadratic formula and factoring, as appropriate to the initial form of the equation. Recognize when the quadratic formula gives complex solutions and write them as $a \pm bi$ for real numbers a and b.	15	SR	9–4
Solve systems of equations			
A.REI.C.6 Solve systems of linear equations exactly and approximately (e.g., with graphs), focusing on pairs of linear equations in two variables.	33 47	CR CR	6–2 6–2
Represent and solve equations and inequalities graphically			
A.REI.D.10 Understand that the graph of an equation in two variables is the set of all its solutions plotted in the coordinate plane, often forming a curve (which could be a straight line).	5	SR	4–3
A.REI.D.11 Explain why the x-coordinates of the points where the graphs of the equations $y = f(x)$ and $y = g(x)$ intersect are the solutions of the equation $f(x) = g(x)$; find the solutions approximately, e.g., using technology to graph the functions, make tables of values, or find successive approximations. Include cases where $f(x)$ and/or $g(x)$ are linear, polynomial, rational, absolute value, exponential, and logarithmic functions.	18 24 65A	SR SR ER	6–1 9–8 6–2
A.REI.D.12 Graph the solutions to a linear inequality in two variables as a half-plane (excluding the boundary in the case of a strict inequality), and graph the solution set to a system of linear inequalities in two variables as the intersection of the corresponding half-planes.	28 46	CR CR	6–5 6–5

CCSS Standards	Test Item(s)	Type	Algebra 1 Student Edition Lesson(s)
Understand the concept of a function and use function notation			
F.IF.A.1 Understand that a function from one set (called the domain) to another set (called the range) assigns to each element of the domain exactly one element of the range. If f is a function and x is an element of its domain, then $f(x)$ denotes the output of f corresponding to the input x. The graph of f is the graph of the equation $y = f(x)$.	52 61A 63A	CR ER ER	4–6 4–6 4–5
F.IF.A.2 Use function notation, evaluate functions for inputs in their domains, and interpret statements that use function notation in terms of a context.	4 42 63B	SR CR ER	4–6 4–6 4–6
Interpret functions that arise in applications in terms of the context			
F.IF.B.4 For a function that models a relationship between two quantities, interpret key features of graphs and tables in terms of the quantities, and sketch graphs showing key features given a verbal description of the relationship.	23 50 56A	SR CR ER	3–1 9–1 9–1
F.IF.B.5 Relate the domain of a function to its graph and, where applicable, to the quantitative relationship it describes.	56B	ER	9–1
F.IF.B.6 Calculate and interpret the average rate of change of a function (presented symbolically or as a table) over a specified interval. Estimate the rate of change from a graph.	44 55 61B	CR CR ER	5–1 5–1 5–1
Analyze functions using different representations			
F.IF.C.7.a Graph functions expressed symbolically and show key features of the graph, by hand in simple cases and using technology for more complicated cases. Graph linear and quadratic functions and show intercepts, maxima, and minima.	13 29 62B	SR CR ER	9–4 9–2 9–2
Build a function that models a relationship between two quantities			
F.BF.A.1.a Write a function that describes a relationship between two quantities. Determine an explicit expression, a recursive process, or steps for calculation from a context.	9 53	SR CR	7–8 4–7
F.BF.A.2 Write arithmetic and geometric sequences both recursively and with an explicit formula, use them to model situations, and translate between the two forms.	40	CR	7–8
Build new functions from existing functions			
F.BF.B.3 Identify the effect on the graph of replacing $f(x)$ by $f(x) + k$, $k f(x)$, $f(kx)$, and $f(x + k)$ for specific values of k (both positive and negative); find the value of k given the graphs. Experiment with cases and illustrate an explanation of the effects on the graph using technology.	14 45	SR CR	5–8 5–3CB

CCSS Standards	Test Item(s)	Type	Algebra 1 Student Edition Lesson(s)
Construct and compare linear and exponential models and solve problems			
F.LE.A.1.a Distinguish between situations that can be modeled with linear functions and with exponential functions. Prove that linear functions grow by equal differences over equal intervals, and that exponential functions grow by equal factors over equal intervals.	3	SR	9–7
F.LE.A.1.b Distinguish between situations that can be modeled with linear functions and with exponential functions. Recognize situations in which one quantity changes at a constant rate per unit interval relative to another.	39	CR	5–1
F.LE.A.1.c Distinguish between situations that can be modeled with linear functions and with exponential functions. Recognize situations in which a quantity grows or decays by a constant percent rate per unit interval relative to another.	38	CR	7–7
Interpret expressions for functions in terms of the situation they model			
F.LE.B.5 Interpret the parameters in a linear or exponential function in terms of a context.	58B	ER	11–7
Summarize, represent, and interpret data on a single count or measurement variable			
S.ID.A.3 Interpret differences in shape, center, and spread in the context of the data sets, accounting for possible effects of extreme data points (outliers).	30 48	CR CR	12–3 12–3
S.ID.A.4 Use the mean and standard deviation of a data set to fit it to a normal distribution and to estimate population percentages. Recognize that there are data sets for which such a procedure is not appropriate. Use calculators, spreadsheets, and tables to estimate areas under the normal curve.	49	CR	12–3
Summarize, represent, and interpret data on two categorical and quantitative variables			
S.ID.B.6.a Represent data on two quantitative variables on a scatter plot, and describe how the variables are related. Fit a function to the data; use functions fitted to data to solve problems in the context of the data.	57A	ER	5–7
S.ID.B.6.c Represent data on two quantitative variables on a scatter plot, and describe how the variables are related. Fit a linear function for a scatter plot that suggests a linear association.	35 57B	CR ER	5–7 5–7
Interpret linear models			
S.ID.C.7 Interpret the slope (rate of change) and the intercept (constant term) of a linear model in the context of the data.	59A	ER	5–7
S.ID.C.8 Compute (using technology) and interpret the correlation coefficient of a linear fit.	43 59B	CR ER	5–7 5–7
S.ID.C.9 Distinguish between correlation and causation.	19 37 54	SR CR CR	5–7 5–7 5–7

About Performance-Based Assessments

Starting in the 2014–2015 school year, students will likely be taking a new assessment that will assess their mastery of their state standards and determine their readiness for college or career work. This new assessment is expected to include Performance-Based Assessments or Performance Tasks.

With the Performance-Based Assessments, students will be expected to show not only their mastery of mathematical concepts and skills that they have learned up through Algebra 1, but also their proficiency with the Standards for Mathematical Practice, including their skills at making sense of problems and developing a solution plan to solve them, at reasoning abstractly and quantitatively, and at developing mathematical models to represent problem situations. These real-world problems will be multi-part, complex tasks.

Students will be given two (or more) class periods to complete these tasks that will require students to analyze given information, and based on their analysis, students will be expected to make decisions about options presented, develop mathematical or visual models to represent problem situations, and present and defend solutions to the problem situation presented. Students should expect to be asked to defend their decisions and justify their models. Writing will be an important element of these tasks.

You will find four (4) practice Performance Tasks to help your students begin to prepare for these new assessments. For each Performance Task, you will find a scoring rubric in the Answers section that you can use to evaluate students' work.

Performance Task: Choosing a Movie-Rental Plan

Complete this performance task in the space provided. Fully answer all parts of the performance task with detailed responses. You should provide sound mathematical reasoning to support your work.

You are considering three different ways to rent movies.

Plan A: Rent DVDs from a kiosk in a nearby grocery store for $1.50 each. The selection of movies is limited.

Plan B: Stream unlimited movies to your computer or TV for $10 per month. The selection of movies is good.

Plan C: Rent DVDs by mail for a $5 monthly fee plus $2 per movie. The selection of movies is outstanding.

Task Description

Choose the movie-rental plan that you think is best. Consider the cost of each plan, the selection offered, and how you like to receive and watch movies.

a. Write functions $A(x)$, $B(x)$, and $C(x)$ that give the cost to rent x movies per month for Plans A, B, and C, respectively.

Performance Task: Choosing a Movie-Rental Plan (continued)

b. If you consider only cost, under what condition does it make sense to choose Plan B over Plan A?

c. If you consider only cost, under what condition does it make sense to choose Plan C over Plan B?

d. Show that Plan A is always more cost-effective than Plan C. Does that mean that Plan A is a better choice than Plan C for everyone? Explain.

e. Which movie-rental plan would you choose? Justify your answer.

Name _____ Class _____ Date _____

Performance Task: Expanding a Parking Lot

Complete this performance task in the space provided. Fully answer all parts of the performance task with detailed responses. You should provide sound mathematical reasoning to support your work.

A high school has a rectangular parking lot that measures 600 ft long by 400 ft wide. The school board wants to double the area of the lot by increasing both its length and width by the same amount, x ft. The board also wants to build a fence around the new lot. The cost to expand the lot is estimated to be $2 per square foot of new space. The cost to fence the lot is estimated to be $30 per foot of fencing. Costs include materials and labor.

Task Description

Estimate the total cost of expanding and fencing in the lot.

a. Draw a diagram of the situation. Your diagram should show both the original parking lot and what the lot will look like after it has been expanded. Label all dimensions.

b. Write an equation that you can use to find x. Solve the equation for x.

Performance Task: Expanding a Parking Lot (continued)

c. What is the area of the new portion of the parking lot that needs to be built? What is the perimeter of the new parking lot?

d. What is the estimated cost of expanding and fencing in the lot?

e. The school has only enough money to pay for half the estimated cost from part (d). The school board plans to raise the remaining funds by selling parking stickers for $100 to students and $200 to faculty. How many student stickers and how many faculty stickers must the school sell? Is there only one possible answer? Explain.

Performance Task: Projectile Motion

Complete this performance task in the space provided. Fully answer all parts of the performance task with detailed responses. You should provide sound mathematical reasoning to support your work.

Suppose an object is launched at an angle of 45° with respect to horizontal. The object's height y (in feet) after it has traveled a horizontal distance of x feet is given by the equation

$$y = -\frac{g}{v^2}x^2 + x + y_0$$

where v is the object's initial speed (in feet per second), y_0 is the object's initial height (in feet), and $g \approx 32$ ft/s^2 is the acceleration due to gravity.

Task Description

You throw a baseball at a 45° angle to your friend standing 100 ft away. Your friend holds her glove 5 ft above the ground to catch the ball. At what initial height, and with what initial speed, should you release the ball so that your friend can catch it without moving her glove?

a. Suppose you release the baseball with an initial height of 6 ft and an initial speed of 50 ft/s. Write and graph an equation that represents the ball's path. Does the ball land in your friend's glove? Explain.

Performance Task: Projectile Motion (continued)

b. If your friend catches the ball, what point must lie on the graph of the ball's path? (Assume you are standing at the point (0, 0).)

c. Use your answer to part (b) to write an equation that describes the initial heights and initial speeds for which your friend catches the ball. Explain why there is more than one initial height and initial speed that work.

d. Find an initial height and an initial speed for which your friend catches the ball. How can you check your answer?

Performance Task: Calculating Inflation

Complete this performance task in the space provided. Fully answer all parts of the performance task with detailed responses. You should provide sound mathematical reasoning to support your work.

The inflation rate for an item (such as a carton of eggs) measures how rapidly the price of the item has changed over time. If an item's price changes from p_1 to p_2 over a period of n years, then the annual inflation rate r (expressed as a decimal) is given by this equation:

$$r = \left(\frac{p_2}{p_1}\right)^{\frac{1}{n}} - 1$$

For example, if the price of an item increases from $2 to $3 over 5 years, then the annual inflation rate is:

$$r = \left(\frac{3}{2}\right)^{\frac{1}{5}} - 1 \approx 1.084 - 1 = 0.084 = 8.4\%$$

The table below shows the average retail prices of several foods in the United States for the years 2000 and 2009.

Food	Price in 2000	Price in 2009
Bread (1 lb)	$0.99	$1.39
Butter (1 lb)	$2.80	$2.67
Cheddar cheese (1 lb)	$3.76	$4.55
Eggs, large (1 dozen)	$0.96	$1.77
Ground beef (1 lb)	$1.63	$2.19
Oranges (1 lb)	$0.62	$0.93
Peanut butter (1 lb)	$1.96	$2.10
Meat cutlets (1 lb)	$3.46	$3.29
Tomatoes (1 lb)	$1.57	$1.96

Task Description

Identify the foods in the table with the least and greatest annual rates of inflation for the period 2000–2009. Then predict the cost in 2015 of the groceries in a basket containing one of each food item from the table.

Name _____ Class _____ Date _____

Performance Task: Calculating Inflation (continued)

a. Find the annual inflation rate for each food in the table for the period 2000–2009. Round your answers to the nearest tenth of a percent.

b. Which food had the least inflation rate? Which had the greatest inflation rate?

c. Which foods, if any, had a negative annual inflation rate? What does a negative annual inflation rate mean?

d. Can you add the percentages of each item to determine the inflation rate for a basket of groceries? Explain.

e. What was the annual inflation rate for a basket of all the food items for the period 2000–2009?

f. Predict the cost of the groceries in the basket in 2015. Explain how you determined your prediction.

SAT/ACT: Introduction

Each year, as a key step in their advancement toward college, more than two million high school students take the SAT Reasoning Test (SAT[*])[1] and the American College Test (ACT).[2] Many also take the more modest counterparts of these tests, the Preliminary SAT Reasoning Test (PSAT/NMSQT)[1] and the Preliminary American College Test, now known as PLAN.[2]

Experts disagree as to how well the SAT and the ACT predict college performance. However fair or unfair it may be, most colleges base their decisions on whether or not to accept a student, at least to some degree, on the student's SAT or ACT score. (PSAT/NMSQT scores are used to qualify students for National Merit Scholarships. Most students take the PSAT/NMSQT and PLAN, however, as practice for the SAT and ACT.) In general, the larger the college, the more importance it places on SAT or ACT test scores in assessing its applicants. Also, the more demanding a college's academic standards, the higher the test scores it expects of its applicants.

Whichever colleges you apply to, your high school transcript and activities, your college application form and supporting materials, and often letters of recommendation and personal interviews will have the greatest influence on whether you are accepted. Still, it's to your advantage to achieve the highest score that you can on the SAT or ACT. This section was designed in three parts to help you meet that goal on the math portions of the two tests.

The first part will tell you what you need to know about the two tests so that you won't be surprised when you sit down on test day and open your booklet. The second part will provide you with a host of test-taking tips. The third part is an SAT/ACT Practice Test you can take to apply what you've learned. If you feel you need more work with specific math content, you can turn to your textbook for a more comprehensive discussion of the relevant mathematics or for extra practice.

In the weeks leading up to whichever test you plan to take, you should spend a set amount of time each day preparing for it. Review key math topics, familiarize yourself with the test formats, and practice the test-taking skills described in this book. Of course, there's no telling how much your preparations will improve your score. Given the importance of the results, however, you have nothing to lose in preparing yourself fully for the test, and a great deal to gain.

[1] SAT is a registered trademark of, and the PSAT is a trademark owned by the College Board, which was not involved in the production of, and does not endorse, this product.

[2] ACT Assessment and the PLAN are registered trademarks owned by ACT, Inc., which was not involved in the production of, and does not endorse, this product.

SAT/ACT: Highlights

The SAT and PSAT/NMSQT

The SAT takes 3 hours and 45 minutes. There are three sections in the math portion of the test.

Section	Length	Type of Question
I	25 minutes	Multiple-Choice
II	25 minutes	Multiple-Choice Grid-Ins
III	20 minutes	Multiple-Choice
Total	70 minutes	

The question types (multiple-choice and grid-ins) will be described later.

In each math section of the test, questions increase gradually in difficulty, with relatively easy questions in the first third of the section and relatively hard ones in the last third.

In addition to the sections listed above, there is a 25-minute "experimental" section, containing new SAT math, critical reading, or writing multiple choice questions that are being tried out. This section is not scored.

The PSAT/NMSQT is similar to the SAT, except that it only lasts for about two hours. In the math portion of the PSAT/NMSQT, the SAT's 20-minute, 16-question section is left out. There is no experimental section.

Both tests cover Knowledge of Number and Operations; Algebra, and Functions; Geometry and Measurement; and Statistics, Probability, and Data Analysis. You are not expected to know the fine details of math. Naturally, the more you know, the more likely you are to do well in the test. The SAT and PSAT/NMSQT, however, emphasize math reasoning and problem solving rather than comprehensive proficiency in mathematics.

The quadratic formula is one example of a fine detail. Neither the SAT nor the PSAT/NMSQT requires you to know it. To solve quadratic equations on the tests, you can use factoring or other elementary methods. Of course, if you *do* know the quadratic formula, you might find it useful, either to solve a problem or to check an answer. In general, however, you're better off using logic and clear reasoning to solve problems, rather than advanced mathematics.

You're allowed to bring a calculator to either test—in fact, you're encouraged to do so. None of the questions will *require* the use of a calculator. On the average, however, students who use calculators wisely do slightly better than students who do not use them at all, and considerably better than students who use them unwisely.

SAT/ACT: Highlights

Scoring

Multiple-choices are scored using the following guidelines: you receive one point for a correct answer and no points if you leave an answer blank. If you answer incorrectly, there's a penalty:

- one-fourth of a point is subtracted from your score if the question has five answer choices.

With grid-ins, you receive one point for a correct answer and no points for an incorrect or blank answer.

Here's how one SAT test was scored:

44 multiple-choice questions

28 correct	=	28 points
12 incorrect (5 answer choices)	=	$(-)$ 3 points $\qquad (12 \times \frac{1}{4} = 3)$
4 blank	=	0 points

10 grid-in questions

6 correct	=	6 points
3 incorrect	=	0 points
1 blank	=	0 points
Raw Score	=	**31 points**

The policy of subtracting a fraction of a point for incorrect answers on multiple-choice questions is called a "guessing penalty."

The raw score is now rounded to the nearest point and converted to a "scaled" score between 200 and 800 (SAT), or 20 and 80 (PSAT/NMSQT). There are no passing or failing scores.

About a month after you take either test, you'll receive your results. These consist of your scaled score and a "percentile" score. The percentile score allows you to compare your results with those of all the other students who took the test. A score in the 64th percentile means that you did better than 64 percent of the people who took the test. The average SAT math score nationwide is 500 points.

SAT/ACT: Highlights

Question Types

There are two types of questions on the math section of the SAT.

Multiple-Choice Questions

Five answers are given for each multiple-choice question. Decide on the correct choice and fill in the corresponding oval on the answer sheet.

If 2 cans of tomatoes weigh 28 ounces, what is the weight, in ounces, of 7 cans of tomatoes?

(A) 2   (B) 8   (C) 56   (D) 98   (E) 196   Ⓐ Ⓑ Ⓒ ● Ⓔ

Grid-In Questions

Grid-in questions are called "student-produced responses" on the test. Each requires you to calculate the correct answer to a question and then write it on the answer grid. Gridding an answer incorrectly will result in a zero score even if your answer is correct. For that reason, you should review the method for gridding answers *before* you take the test, because there are several ways to grid incorrectly. The following pages will give you a chance to do that.

Sample Grids

Your responses are recorded on a special answer grid that provides ways of showing decimal points and fraction bars. You will be able to code decimal and fraction answers. For example, a student who gets an answer of 23.9 on a problem would code the answer as shown in this grid.

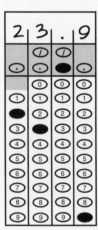

The grid is composed of four columns. If you look closely, you will notice that along with the digits 0 through 9, the division sign (/) and the decimal point (.) are available. *The first column cannot be filled with 0 or /.* Also, each character in the answer must occupy a single column in the grid. So the answer 23.9 requires all four available columns. Notice that there is no provision in the grid structure for coding negative values. *This is a clear message that there will be no questions in this part of the test that have negative answers.*

SAT/ACT: Highlights

The ACT and PLAN

The ACT takes three and one-half hours. The math section of the test lasts one hour and consists of 60 multiple-choice questions. Questions are arranged roughly in order of difficulty, from easiest to hardest. As with the SAT, you may use a calculator on the ACT.

Scoring

Unlike the SAT, the ACT is not scored by deducting a fraction of your incorrect answers from your correct ones. You get one point for a correct answer and no points for either an incorrect answer or an answer left blank. There is no penalty for guessing.

Here's how one ACT test was scored:

60 multiple-choice questions

38 correct	=	38 points
22 incorrect	=	0 points
Raw Score	**=**	**38 points**

The content of ACT test questions is invariable. There are always

- 24 questions on pre-algebra and elementary algebra;
- 18 questions on intermediate algebra and coordinate geometry;
- 14 questions on geometry;
- 4 questions on basic trigonometry.

The PLAN is a mini-ACT. The math section of the test lasts 40 minutes and consists of 40 multiple-choice questions, apportioned as follows:

- 14 questions on pre-algebra;
- 8 questions on elementary algebra;
- 7 questions on coordinate geometry;
- 11 questions on plane geometry.

As on the ACT, you can use a calculator when you take the PLAN.

Getting Your Results

You'll receive your ACT results in four to six weeks. Your math score (and your score in each of the other three areas of the test) will be a number from 1 to 36; 36 will be the highest possible score. (The PLAN is scored from 1 to 32.) As with the SAT, you'll also receive a percentile ranking so that you can compare your results with those of other students who took the test.

SAT/ACT: Test-Taking Tips

Taking the Test

The following are time-honored test-taking strategies.

Manage Your Time Efficiently.

The questions in each section of the test are arranged roughly in order of difficulty. As you begin, make a quick estimate of the average amount of time you have to answer each question. Use the estimate to guide you through the section. Allow yourself a little less than the average amount of time for the early, easier first questions so that you'll have extra time for the harder ones later on.

Starting with the first question, move as quickly as you can through the section. Consider each question in turn. Make a quick assessment as to whether you can solve it rapidly. If you think you can, do so. Work at a comfortable pace, but don't linger. Spending too much time on a problem in the fanciful belief that you've *almost got it* is a killer. Remember: all problems are worth the same number of points. You receive one point for each easy question that you answer correctly and one point for each hard one. How should you spend your time?

If you decide that you can probably solve a problem with a little more time, draw a circle around it. After you've made your first pass through all the questions, answering those that seem easy, return to the questions you've circled. This second look is often successful, so don't get discouraged if you find yourself circling lots of questions. Continue to pace yourself during the second pass. Work your way through the questions you think you have a chance on, but don't be reluctant to abandon them again and move on if they continue to tie you up. After the second pass, return to the questions that continue to stump you if time remains.

If you're sure that you won't be able to solve a problem, draw an **X** beside it and forget it. Throwing in the towel on questions you can't answer is simply good time management and nothing to apologize for. No one is expected to answer every question correctly and few people do.

Be careful.

Beware of the following:

- Under the pressure of test-taking, it's easy to make careless mistakes. Work through calculations methodically, rechecking them quickly at the end. Ask yourself if answers are reasonable. Is the price after a discount greater than the original price? Does one of the acute angles in a right triangle measure 150°? Use estimation whenever possible. On multiple-choice questions, an estimate may be enough to help you decide which of the given answers is correct without actually working it out.

- On multiple-choice questions, watch out for "obvious" choices. In the first part of a section, where the questions are relatively easy, an answer that seems obvious may be the right one. But in the last part, the obvious answer may have been put there to deceive you. After all, if an answer is obvious, what's the question doing in the hard part of the test?

SAT/ACT: Test-Taking Tips

- Check and double-check to make sure that you're writing your answers in the correct spots, and beside the correct numbers. To guard against potential disasters, many students write all their answers in their test booklets *only*, transferring them all at once to their answer sheets in the final minute or two.

- Beware of long computations. SAT and ACT problems can usually be solved with minimal calculations. If you find yourself in the midst of a multi-step nightmare, it's best to stop and look for a shortcut—or move on to the next question.

- If you're told that a figure is not drawn to scale, believe it. Don't assume that lengths and angles are drawn accurately.

- Measurements may be given in different units. If they are, convert and work the problem in one unit.

Be smart.

Use these ideas to simplify your work and improve your score.

- Write in your test booklet. There's no reward for a clean booklet and no penalty for one that's covered with pencil marks. If a question doesn't have a drawing and one would help, draw it. Write measurements and values on the drawing. When you calculate an answer, write out your calculations so that you can check them later. The next time, try doing them a different way. This is a good way to check your work and often reveals careless mistakes.

- On multiple-choice questions, draw a line through choices you know to be wrong. This will simplify the job of choosing the right answer.

- Look at the answer choices before working a problem. This will show you the form of the answer that is required (a fraction, for example), allowing you to work the problem in that form from the beginning rather than having to rewrite your answer later in a different form.

- Under "Reference Information," the SAT booklet provides a considerable amount of information on geometrical relationships. Use it.

- Know commonly used numbers. Recognize powers of 2, 3, and 5. Know the decimal equivalents for simple fractions with denominators of 2, 3, 4, 5, 6, 8, and 10. Know the common Pythagorean triples 3-4-5 and 5-12-13 and recognize their multiples.

SAT/ACT: Practice Test

Section I Multiple Choice

In the following problems you have five choices for an answer. Only one choice is correct. Mark your answer by filling in the correct bubble on the answer sheet that your teacher provides.

1. $\dfrac{42}{25} \times \dfrac{25}{42} =$

(A) $\dfrac{1}{2}$

(B) $\dfrac{3}{4}$

(C) 1

(D) 2

(E) $\dfrac{5}{2}$

If 6 is added to 2 times a number, the result is 3 less than the number.

3. Which of the following equations represents the statement above?

(A) $6 + 2 \times n = 3 - n$

(B) $2n + 6 < 3n$

(C) $6 = 2n - 3 + n$

(D) $2n + 6 = n - 3$

(E) $2n + 6 + 3 < n$

2. The price of an $8.00 calculator is lowered 20%. What is the new price?

(A) $1.60

(B) $3.20

(C) $4.80

(D) $6.40

(E) $8.00

$\{60, 62, 64, ..., 116, 118, 120\}$

4. How many members are there in the set of even numbers from 60 to 120 inclusive?

(A) 15

(B) 29

(C) 30

(D) 31

(E) 45

GO ON

SAT/ACT: Practice Test

Section I Multiple Choice (continued)

---

5. *a* is a factor of 44. *b* is a factor of 27. Which number below could *not* be a value for *ab*?

(A) 6

(B) 18

(C) 20

(D) 36

(E) 99

---

7. The sales tax on an $18 meal is $0.90. At that rate, what would be the sales tax on a $30 meal?

(A) $1.80

(B) $1.50

(C) $1.44

(D) $0.60

(E) $0.54

---

6. Bookshelves sell for $4.49. If you buy in quantity, the cost is reduced to $3.99 per shelf. How much do you save if you buy 50 shelves at the lower price?

(A) $209.50

(B) $199.50

(C) $29.50

(D) $25.00

(E) $15.00

---

8. Simplify: $\dfrac{2}{6} \cdot \dfrac{4}{8} \cdot \dfrac{6}{10} \cdot \dfrac{8}{12}$.

(A) $\dfrac{1}{15}$

(B) $\dfrac{1}{8}$

(C) $\dfrac{3}{11}$

(D) $\dfrac{1}{2}$

(E) $\dfrac{5}{9}$

GO ON

SAT/ACT: Practice Test

Section I Multiple Choice (continued)

---

9. If $\dfrac{x + 5}{x - 5} = 2$, then $x - 5 =$

(A) -5

(B) 0

(C) 5

(D) 10

(E) 15

---

11. If $m = 3$ and $n = -2$, what is the value of $-2(m - n) + n^3$?

(A) -4

(B) -10

(C) -12

(D) -16

(E) -18

---

10. If $|x + 1| = 5$, then $x =$

(A) 4 only

(B) 4 or -4

(C) -4 only

(D) -6 only

(E) -6 or 4

---

12. In the Drama Club, there are 9 students aged 15, 7 students aged 16, 11 students aged 17, and 4 students aged 18. Which of the following statements about the ages of the students is true:

  I. The mode is 17.
  II. The median is 16.
  III. The mean is 15.

(A) I and II

(B) I and III

(C) II and III

(D) I, II, and III

(E) None

GO ON

SAT/ACT: Practice Test

Section I Multiple Choice (continued)

13. The area of a circle is 100π. The diameter is

(A) 10

(B) 10π

(C) 31.4

(D) 20

(E) 20π

Not drawn to scale.

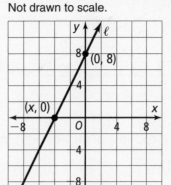

15. The slope of line ℓ is 2. $x =$

(A) −16

(B) −4

(C) 2

(D) 4

(E) 16

14. Simplify $\dfrac{20 + x}{20}$.

(A) x

(B) $1 + x$

(C) $1 + \dfrac{x}{20}$

(D) $20 + x$

(E) $20 + \dfrac{x}{20}$

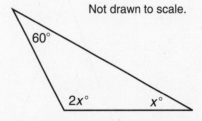

Not drawn to scale.

16. What is x in the above figure?

(A) 20°

(B) 25°

(C) 30°

(D) 40°

(E) 60°

GO ON

SAT/ACT: Practice Test

Section I Multiple Choice (continued)

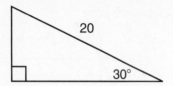

17. What is the area of the above triangle?

(A) $10\sqrt{3}$

(B) $20\sqrt{3}$

(C) $50\sqrt{3}$

(D) $100\sqrt{3}$

(E) $200\sqrt{3}$

19. Four small congruent equilateral triangles are placed together to form a larger equilateral triangle. Write the ratio
$$\frac{\text{perimeter of small triangle}}{\text{perimeter of large triangle}}.$$

(A) $\dfrac{1}{6}$

(B) $\dfrac{1}{4}$

(C) $\dfrac{1}{3}$

(D) $\dfrac{1}{2}$

(E) $\dfrac{2}{3}$

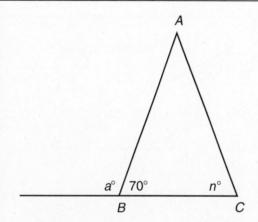

18. In the figure above, $AB = AC$. What is the sum of $a + n$?

(A) 180

(B) 190

(C) 200

(D) 210

(E) Cannot be determined

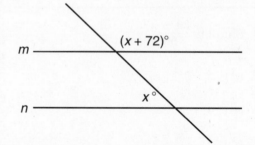

20. Lines m and n are parallel. $x =$

(A) 9

(B) 36

(C) 54

(D) 60

(E) 64

GO ON

SAT/ACT: Practice Test

Section I Multiple Choice (continued)

21. What is the y-intercept of the line
$ax + by = c$?

(A) $\dfrac{a}{b}$

(B) $-\dfrac{a}{b}$

(C) c

(D) $\dfrac{c}{b}$

(E) $-abc$

22. Find the distance from $(-4, 4)$ to the intersection of the lines.

$x + y = 7$
$x - y = 9$

(A) 4

(B) 5

(C) 10

(D) 12

(E) 13

23. In $\triangle ABC$, C is a right angle, $BC = 12$, and $AC = 16$. $\sin B =$

(A) $\dfrac{4}{5}$

(B) $\dfrac{3}{5}$

(C) $\dfrac{4}{3}$

(D) $\dfrac{5}{4}$

(E) $\dfrac{5}{3}$

24. All of the circle sectors have equal areas, but the labels have been omitted from 5 sectors. If a dart strikes each board randomly, the probability of hitting D or E is $\dfrac{1}{4}$. How many of the 5 blank sectors should be labeled E?

(A) 1

(B) 2

(C) 3

(D) 4

(E) 5

GO ON

SAT/ACT: Practice Test

Section I Multiple Choice (continued)

25. Which of the following is the midpoint of $(4, 8)$ and $(-2, 1)$?

(A) $\left(3, \dfrac{7}{2}\right)$

(B) $\left(1, \dfrac{9}{2}\right)$

(C) $\left(3, \dfrac{9}{2}\right)$

(D) $\left(6, -\dfrac{1}{2}\right)$

(E) none of the above

26. Which of the following expressions is *not* equivalent to $2\sqrt{3} + 3\sqrt{2}$?

(A) $7\sqrt{3} + 19\sqrt{2} - 5\sqrt{3} - 16\sqrt{2}$

(B) $\sqrt{3 \cdot 4} + \sqrt{2 \cdot 9}$

(C) $\sqrt{12} + \sqrt{18}$

(D) $\sqrt{\dfrac{36}{3}} + \sqrt{\dfrac{36}{2}}$

(E) $5\sqrt{\dfrac{3}{2}}$

27. In an inverse variation, the constant of variation is 6. When $y = \dfrac{1}{2}$, which of the following is x?

(A) $\dfrac{1}{3}$

(B) $\dfrac{13}{2}$

(C) 3

(D) 12

(E) none of the above

28. Which of the following lists all of the values excluded from the domain of $y = \dfrac{3}{x^3 - 4x}$?

(A) $x = 2$ and $x = -2$

(B) $x = 0$ and $x = 2$

(C) $x = \dfrac{1}{4}$

(D) $x = 2$, $x = 0$, and $x = -2$

(E) $x = 0$ and $x = 4$

GO ON

SAT/ACT: Practice Test

Section I Multiple Choice (continued)

29. Which of the following is the lowest common denominator of $\dfrac{1}{2y^2 - 11y - 21}$ and $\dfrac{3}{y - 7}$?

(A) $(y - 7)(2y + 3)$

(B) $(y - 7)(2y^2 - 11y - 21)$

(C) $(y - 7)$

(D) $2y^3 - 25y^2 + 56y + 147$

(E) none of the above

30. Which of the following is the solution of $\dfrac{3}{a} - \dfrac{16}{a^2} = 2$?

(A) $a > 0$

(B) $a = -\dfrac{14}{3}$

(C) $a = 16$

(D) $2a^2 - 3a + 16 = 0$

(E) none of the above

31. Which of the following equations models exponential decay?

(A) $y = \dfrac{1}{4} \cdot 500^x$

(B) $\dfrac{1}{3}y = 6 \cdot 100^x$

(C) $y = 0.5 \cdot 8^x$

(D) $y = 23 \cdot \left(\dfrac{1}{2}\right)^x$

(E) $y = 0.004 \cdot 2^x$

32. Which of the following is true?

(A) $\dfrac{x^{-3}}{x} = \dfrac{x}{x^4}$

(B) $\dfrac{y^2}{y^0}$ is undefined

(C) $\dfrac{b^5 c^{-2} d^4}{b^6 c d^{-2}} = \dfrac{d^8}{bc^3}$

(D) $\dfrac{f^2 g^{-3} h^3}{f^4 g^2 h^{-4}} = \dfrac{h^7}{f^2 g^5}$

(E) none of the above

STOP

SAT/ACT: Practice Test

Section II Student-Produced Responses

After you solve each problem on this section, enter your answer on the corresponding grid provided on your answer sheet.

---

1. In $\triangle ABC$, $\angle A$ is 6 times the measure of $\angle C$, and $\angle C$ is twice the measure of $\angle B$. What is the measure of $\angle B$?

2. A square with sides equal to 6 has the same area as a triangle with a base of 9. What is the height of the triangle?

3. Mrs. M drove 10 minutes at 60 miles per hour, then 20 minutes at 30 miles per hour. For the rest of the hour, she drove at a rate that put her 48 miles from her starting point. What was that rate?

4. 1,024 divided by 32^2 equals what power of 2?

SAT/ACT: Practice Test

Section II Student-Produced Responses (continued)

---

5. The hypotenuse of a 30°-60°-90° triangle is $10\sqrt{2}$. To the nearest whole number, what is the length of the triangle's shorter leg?

7. Five cards are labeled 0, 2, 4, 6, and 8. Two cards are picked without replacement. What is the probability that their product is 0?

---

6. In one town last year there was a ratio of 1 recreational vehicle to every 2 trucks. This year there are the same number of trucks but 200 more recreational vehicles, and the ratio is now 1 to 1. How many trucks are there this year?

8. MARCHING BAND CONTEST RESULTS

	1st Place (6 points)	2nd Place (4 points)	3rd Place (2 points)
Musical Quality		B	
Originality	A	C	
Marching Quality			C

This score card for the three schools A, B, and C is incomplete. What is one possible total score for School B?

SAT/ACT: Practice Test

Section II Student-Produced Responses (continued)

9. The average of six consecutive even integers is 31. What is the sum of the smallest plus the largest of the integers?

10. $0.86^2 - 0.84^2 =$

STOP

Week 1

1. A

2. C

3. 6766

4. No; Answers will vary. Sample: A real number can be a whole number, a decimal, or a fraction. An integer is the set of whole numbers and their opposites. If I add two fractions or two decimals, the result is usually not an integer. Example: $5.6 + 2.1 = 7.7$

Week 2

1. A

2. C

3. a. $w = 5h$;

Hours	Wages
2	10
3	15
4	20
5	25

b. 5 hours.

4. a.

x	0	1	2	3	4	5
y	55	60	65	70	75	80

b. $y = 5x + 55$

c.

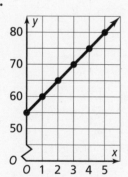

d. Answers may vary. Sample: The table, graph, and equation may represent a temperature that starts at 55 degrees and increases by 5 degrees each hour for 5 hours.

Week 3

1. A

2. B

3. $m\angle A = 16$, $m\angle B = m\angle C = 82$.

4. Students should use the bank to complete the table.

Steps	Reasons
$-\dfrac{2}{5}(x + 5) - 3 = 65$	Original equation
$-\dfrac{2}{5}(x) - \dfrac{2}{5}(5) - 3 = 65$	Distributive Property
$-\dfrac{2}{5}x + (-2) - 3 = 65$	Use multiplication to simplify.
$-\dfrac{2}{5}x - 5 = 65$	Simplify using addition.
$-\dfrac{2}{5}x = 70$	Add 5 to each side and simplify.
$x = -175$	Multiply each side by $\dfrac{5}{2}$ and simplify.

Week 4

1. C

2. 13 kg

3. a. $30x - 640 = 25x - 450$

b. $x = 38$

Week 5

1. A

2. D

3. The skyscraper is 295.2 m tall.

4. a. $165, $176.47
b. The 15% discount saves the customer $26.47, which is far more than the money saved with the flat discount of $15.

Week 6

1. C

2. D

3. $-3(g + 5) > 3$
$-3g - 15 > 3$ Distributive Property
$-3g > 18$ Add 15 to each side.
$g < -6$ Division Property of Inequalities

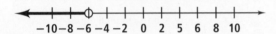

4. a. $l = 2w + 3$
$2l + 2w \le 78$
$2(2w + 3) + 2w \le 78$
$w \le 12$

The width of the rectangle must be 12 feet or less to meet the conditions of the problem. Because width must be a measure greater than zero, the possible solutions are all widths greater than zero and less than or equal to 12.

Week 7

1. A

2. $x = -6$ or $x = -10$;

He needs between 15 and 25 people to contribute.

3. a. $200 \le 50 + 10p \le 300$

b.

Week 8

1. C

2. a.

$h = 3w + 2$	
w	h
1	5
2	8
3	11
4	14
5	17

b. 26 cm

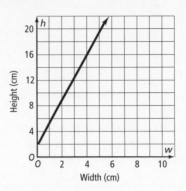
Width (cm)

3. a. $c = m + 4$

b. 11 miles

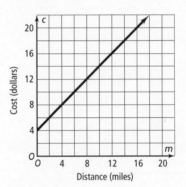
Distance (miles)

Week 9

1. D

2. a. Domain: {7, 14};   **b.** Range: {10, 17, 24, 31};
c. The relation is NOT a function because values in the domain correspond to more than one value in the range.

3. a. $c = 1.50\,g + 1.50$ **b.** $7.50   **c.** 8

Week 10

1. A

2. a. $S(n) = \dfrac{1}{2} + (n - 1)\left(\dfrac{3}{8}\right)$ **b.** $4\dfrac{5}{8}$

3. a. Explicit: $S(n) = 100 + 25n$;
Recursive: $S(0) = 100, S(n) = S(n - 1) + 25$;
b. $475

c. Answers may vary. Sample: I chose the explicit formula because I can substitute any week, or term, into the function and find the value of the account. The recursive function requires that I find each account balance for successive weeks until week 15 to find the value of the account.

Week 11

1. C

2. B

3.

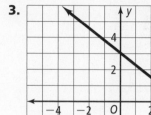

4. a. $y = -15d + 1200$

b.

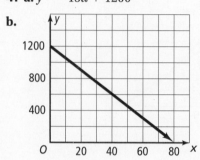

c. The expedition is expected to last 80 days because $d = 80$ when $1200 - 15d = 0$.

Week 12

1. A

2. a.

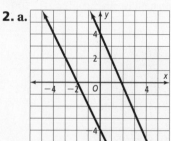

b. $y = -2x - 4$;

3.

Possible Equation of the Line Drawn	NOT an Equation of the Line Drawn
$y - 8 = \frac{1}{2}(x - 4)$	$y - 4 = \frac{1}{2}(x - 8)$
$y - 1 = \frac{1}{2}(x + 10)$	$y + 10 = 2(x - 1)$
	$y + 10 = \frac{1}{2}(x - 1)$

Week 13

1. C

2. Neither; the slope of the first line is $\frac{-2}{5}$ and the slope of the second line is $\frac{5}{6}$.

3. a. $y = 15x - 200$, where y is the total profit and x is the number of tutoring sessions in one month. Total profit for the month is $1000.

b.

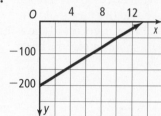

The graph models the profit per month y after tutoring students for x hours. The x-intercept is at 13.3 because that is where the business breaks even and starts to make a profit.

Week 14

1. D

2. a.

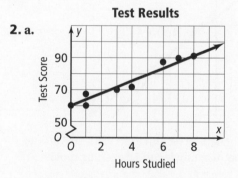

b. Answers may vary. Sample: 80. Check students' work.

3. a.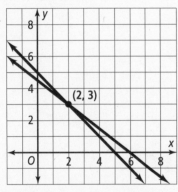

b. The correlation coefficient is -0.985.

c. There seems to be both a correlation and causation. There is a negative correlation between the number of active hours and the students' body mass index. It seems to show that the more active hours spent causes the body mass index to go down.

Week 15

1. A

2. $\left(2, \dfrac{1}{2}\right)$

3. a. $x + y = 5$

$6x + 8y = 36$;

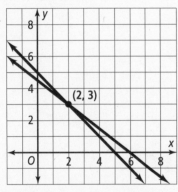

The point of intersection is at $(2, 3)$. So Antonio saw 2 matinee movies and 3 evening movies.

b. The intersection of the graphs of the two functions is the solution because this is the only point where the sum of the matinee movies and number of evening movies is 5 and the total cost is $36.

Week 16

1. D

2.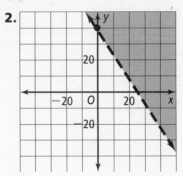

3. a. 25; 10; $2x + 3y = 80$

$x + y = 35$

b.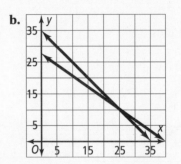

Week 17

1. A

2. Check students' graphs. Answers will vary. Sample: There is no overlap between the shaded areas.

3. a. Answers will vary. Sample: $2x + 3y \geq 500$ and $x > 50$.

b.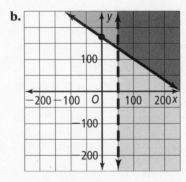

c. Check students' solutions for reasonableness.

Week 18

1. C

2. $24at^{\frac{6}{7}}$ Check students' work

3. Yes, this is correct. Because $y > x$,
$\dfrac{a^x}{a^y} = a^{x-y} = a^{-(y-x)} = \dfrac{1}{a^{(y-x)}}$. Check

students' examples.

Week 19

1. C

2. The number of prairie dogs 5 years before the population was measured.

3. a. $A = 8(1 + 0.15)^t$

b. 229 mice

c.

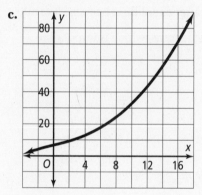

Week 20

1. B

2. a. explicit formula: $a_n = 2^n$; recursive
formula: $a_1 = 2, a_n = 2(a_{n-1})$.

b. The coefficient 2 is the first term in the sequence, which is Brian's first two ancestors or his parents. The nth term is the number of generations he goes back.

3. a. This is an exponential decay situation where the value of the new house starts at \$200,000.00 and decays at a rate of 15% a year.

b. $y = 200,000(1 - 0.15)^x$

c. \$88,741.06.

Week 21

1. B

2. Expressions Equivalent to $2x^2 + 17x$:

$(4x^2 + 10x + 7) - (2x^2 - 7x + 7)$,

$x(2x + 17)$,

$(2x^2 + 5x^2) + (-5x^2 + x + x + 15x)$

Expressions Not Equivalent to $2x^2 + 17x$:
$5x^2 - (3x^2 + 12x) + 5x$

3. a. $3x^2 - 4x - 15$

b. quadratic trinomial

Week 22

1. B

2. $x^3 + 6x^2 + 24x + 32$, cubic polynomial

3. a. $2x^2 + 12x + 18$

b. $3.14x^2 + 18.84x + 28.26$

c. $0.43x^2 + 2.58x + 3.87$

d. 10.75 cm^2

Week 23

1. C

2. $6x + 8$

3. a. Check students' sketches. The length of the garden plus the pathway is $6 + 2x$ and the width is $4 + 2x$. The total area is $(6 + 2x)(4 + 2x)$.

b. The the width of the pathway is 1 m.

Week 24

1. D

2. a.

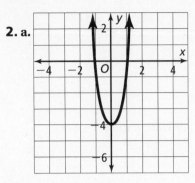

b. $(1, -1)$

3. a. The ball will hit the ground after 3 s, because $x = -1$ and 3. The function increases until $t = 1$. This is the interval that the ball is traveling upward to its maximum height at 1 s. The function then decreases through the t-intercept 3. This is where the ball is falling back toward the ground and hits a height of 0 ft at 3 s.

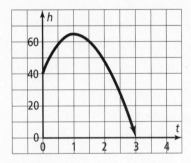

Week 25

1. B, D

2. $x = \pm\sqrt{3} - 2$ or $x = -3.73$ and -0.27

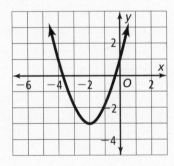

3. a. $2x + 1$

b. The rooftop is a square because the area is $(2x + 1)^2$. So the side lengths are the same.

c. $x = 10$ m

Week 26

1. A

2. A

3. a. $t =$ about 1.25 s and 12.75 s.

b. The solutions are about 1.25 s and 12.75 s, so the bird is under water between those two times.

4. a. $V = 12x^2 - 26x + 10$

b. $x = \dfrac{1}{6}, x = 2$

c. When $x = 2$, $l = 3$ ft and $w = 1$ ft. The solution $x = \dfrac{1}{6}$ is an extraneous solution because it results in negative side lengths, which is impossible.

Week 27

1. D

2. A

3. $x = \dfrac{5 \pm \sqrt{13}}{2}$

4. a. $a = \pm\sqrt{d^2 - 9}$

b. $a = \pm 4$

c. $a = -4$ is an extraneous solution because a negative side length is not reasonable.

Week 28

1. A, D, F

2. a.

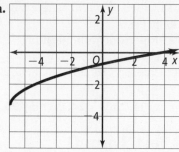

b. domain: $x \geq -5$; range: $y \geq -3$

3. a.

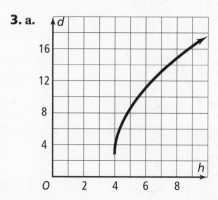

b. height = 20 ft

Week 29

1. C

2.

Graphs with $y = 4$ as Asymptote	Graphs with $x = 6$ as Asymptote	Graphs with Neither $y = 4$ nor $x = 6$ as Asymptotes
$y - 4 = \dfrac{1}{x - 6}$ $y = \dfrac{(x + 2)}{(x + 2)(x - 3)} + 4$	$y - 4 = \dfrac{1}{x - 6}$ $y = \dfrac{4}{x - 6}$	$4y = \dfrac{1}{x + 6}$

3. a. $x^2 - 17x + 30 = 0$; $x = 2$ and $x = 15$.

b. The first root, $x = 2$, does not fit the given situation. If Bill can do the job in 2 days, then Andrew can do the job in -3 days, which does not make sense. Therefore, the solution is that Bill can complete the job in 15 days.

Week 30

1. C

2. a. mean: 7.9, median: 7, mode: 7, range: 12.

b. Answers may vary. Sample: There are no outliers, therefore the mean is the best measure of central tendency.

3. a. 6 : 17; about 35%

b. 6 : 11; about 55%

c. 35 : 89; about 39%

d. 108 : 331; about 33%

e. Overhaul 4 × 4; Mini Buggy

Screening Test

1. D **2.** H **3.** B **4.** H **5.** B **6.** J **7.** A **8.** J
9. C **10.** G **11.** A **12.** J **13.** D **14.** F **15.** A
16. H **17.** C **18.** F **19.** B **20.** J **21.** C **22.** J
23. B **24.** F **25.** C **26.** H **27.** A **28.** J **29.** C
30. H **31.** A **32.** H **33.** B **34.** H **35.** B **36.** J
37. A

Common Core Readiness Assessment 1

1. B **2.** F **3.** B **4.** J **5.** D **6.** G **7.** D
8. H **9.** A **10.** H **11.** A **12.** G **13.** D **14.** H
15. B **16.** F **17.** C **18.** H **19.** B **20.** F **21.** D
22. G **23.** C **24.** H **25.** C **26.** G **27.** A **28.** H
29. D **30.** G

Common Core Readiness Assessment 2

1. C **2.** J **3.** A **4.** F **5.** D **6.** G **7.** D **8.** G
9. C **10.** H **11.** B **12.** H **13.** D **14.** F **15.** D
16. J **17.** C **18.** J **19.** D **20.** F **21.** A **22.** G
23. B **24.** J **25.** B **26.** F **27.** A **28.** H **29.** D
30. H **31.** B

Common Core Readiness Assessment 3

1. D **2.** H **3.** A **4.** G **5.** C **6.** H **7.** B **8.** F **9.** A
10. F **11.** D **12.** H **13.** B **14.** F **15.** C **16.** F
17. D **18.** G **19.** B **20.** F **21.** A **22.** G **23.** B
24. J **25.** A **26.** G **27.** D **28.** J **29.** A **30.** F

Common Core Readiness Assessment 4

1. C **2.** G **3.** B **4.** F **5.** C **6.** J **7.** B **8.** H **9.** B
10. F **11.** C **12.** G **13.** B **14.** F **15.** C **16.** H
17. C **18.** F **19.** A **20.** F **21.** C **22.** H **23.** A
24. J **25.** C **26.** H **27.** B **28.** H **29.** B **30.** G
31. B **32.** F **33.** A **34.** H **35.** C **36.** J **37.** A

Common Core Readiness Assessment 5

1. A **2.** J **3.** B **4.** J **5.** C **6.** G **7.** B **8.** G **9.** B
10. J **11.** B **12.** G **13.** C **14.** G **15.** D **16.** F
17. C **18.** J **19.** C **20.** H **21.** C **22.** H **23.** B
24. F **25.** D **26.** J **27.** C **28.** G **29.** A **30.** H
31. B **32.** F **33.** C **34.** J **35.** D **36.** F
37. C **38.** J

Quarter 1 Test, Form G

1. $12x - 8$ **2.** $A(n) = 1 + 7(n - 1)$
3. $0 \leq t \leq 50$ **4.** 10, 20, 40 **5.** {2, 3, 5, 8}
6. $x = 3.75$ **7.** $14.70 **8.** $c = 12m$, where cost is c
and month is m **9.** ≈ 8
10. Associative Property of Multiplication
11. $n \geq 25$ **12.** $x \leq 5$ **13.** 9 in. **14.** 6
15. Distributive Property **16.** $0.75t = 16.50$; 22
tickets **17.** yes **18.** 8 **19.** 3 **20.** $k = 5$
21. $y = 3$ **22.** $h = -11$ **23.** $\frac{44}{7}$ **24.** 0.3 min **25.** 28

Quarter 2 Test, Form G

1.
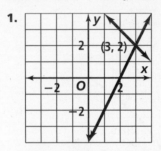

2.
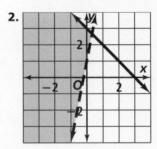

3. $(4, -2)$

4. $\begin{aligned} 25p + 18g &= 265 \\ p + g &= 12 \end{aligned}$; 7 private, 5 group

5. $\begin{aligned} 0.25q + 0.05n &= 1.25 \\ q + n &= 13 \end{aligned}$; 3 quarters, 10 nickels

6.
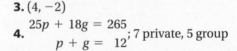

7.

x	$f(x) = -\frac{1}{2}x + 3$	(x, y)
-4	$f(-4) = -\frac{1}{2}(-4) + 3 = 5$	$(-4, 5)$
0	$f(0) = -\frac{1}{2}(0) + 3 = 3$	$(0, 3)$
4	$f(4) = -\frac{1}{2}(4) + 3 = 1$	$(4, 1)$

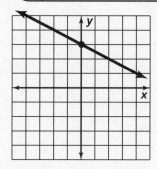

8. $y = 8518 - 223x$; 7626

9. $y + 7 = -\frac{1}{3}(x - 2)$

10. $\{37, 17, 65\}$ **11.** $c(x) = 20 - 0.79x$

12. $y = -2x$ **13.** 18, 21, 24 **14.** 180, 144, 108

15. $y = -\frac{5}{8}x - \frac{3}{8}$ **16.** 5

17. $(0, 6)$; $(4, 0)$ **18.** $y = \frac{3}{5}x - 5$

19. negative correlation

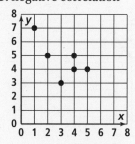

20.

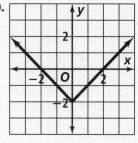

21. $y = \frac{3}{2}x - 3$

22. parallel **23.** yes; The ordered pairs make the inequality true. **24.** Answers may vary, sample: The function shown by the table is one more than $f(x)$.
25. $y = 750 + 25x$; $5.63 per book

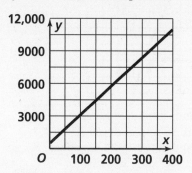

Quarter 3 Test, Form G

1. $\dfrac{a^{\frac{2}{3}}}{b^3}$ **2.** $252x^2y^{12}$ **3.** 3.463×10^9

4. $472, 42.7 \times 10^2, 0.0427 \times 10^7, 4.72 \times 10^5$

5. 6, 12, 24

6.

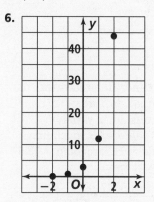

7. 0.75, 1 **8.** ± 5 **9.** $y = 3x^2$; quadratic

10. $4\sqrt{7}$ ft **11.** 4 **12.** $(2, -7)$ **13.** no real

solutions **14.** $5x^4 - 11x^2 - 2x$ **15.** $12x^5 - 15x^2$

16. $y = x^2 + x - 30$; $(0, -30)$ **17.**

$y = (x + 6)(x - 1)$; $x = 1$ and $x = -6$

18. $T = \frac{2}{5}s^2$ **19.** $f(x) = 2 \cdot 3^x$ **20.** 4

21.

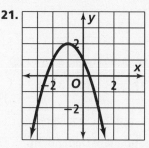

22a.

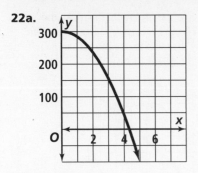

22b. 4.3 seconds
23. For growth, $b > 1$; for decay, $0 < b < 1$.
24. $(-4, 32)$ and $(3, -17)$ **25.** no effect

Quarter 4 Test, Form G

1. $\frac{1}{4}$ **2.** 102

3.

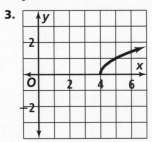

4. The mean of set 2 is 6 more than the mean of set 1. The ranges are equal. **5.** $T(x) = 12/x$
6. 20% **7.** direct; The constant of variation is 0.045. **8.** minimum value = 65; maximum value = 97; first quartile = 71.5; median = 79.5; third quartile = 86.5 **9.** skewed

10. 44 **11.** 9 **12.** $\dfrac{5\sqrt{11} - 5\sqrt{7}}{4}$ **13.** 3, 1

14. vertical asymptote: $x = 3$; horizontal asymptote: $y = 0$

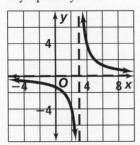

15. The graph will be the same shape, moved up 2 units. **16.** $\dfrac{x + 3}{x(x + 1)}$ **17.** $3x^2 - 2x - 3$ **18.** $\dfrac{4}{25}$

19. -3 **20.** $\dfrac{6}{10}$ or $\dfrac{3}{5}$ **21.** median **22.** 6435 ways
23. 88.1 ft **24.** a. Independent b. Dependent
25. $\sin L = \dfrac{MN}{LM}$; $\tan M = \dfrac{NL}{MN}$

Mid-Course Test, Form G

1. 15 lb/in.^{2} or psi **2.** 1.3% **3.** $t = I/pr$
4. 23.625 **5.** 40 left-handed students
6. The volume will quadruple. **7.** 8 **8.** 5
9. 0 **10.** $y \le 242$ **11.** 22 Q d Q 2

12.

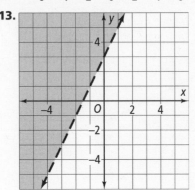

13.

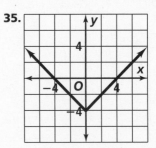

14. $c(k) = 20 - 1.29x$ **15.** $\{-4, -5, 7.25\}$
16. -42 **17.** yes; $-3 > -8$ **18.** no solution
19. $x - 32 = 289.14$; \$321.14 **20.** $\dfrac{2}{3}x = 8$; 12 gallons
21. $2x + 5 = 12$; 3.5 **22.** $2(c + 2) + 3c = 34$ \$8
23. $0.25x \le 2.20$; 8 gumballs **24.** 32% **25.** 287
26. 40 million **27.** $-\dfrac{1}{3}$ **28.** 2 **29.** $y = \dfrac{3}{2}x + 1$
30. $y = 18$ **31.** $y = \dfrac{4}{9}x + \dfrac{17}{9}$ **32.** $y = -\dfrac{1}{3}x$
33. The function represented by the table of values **34.** negative strong correlation

35.

36. $y = |x + 6|$ **37.** 113°F **38.** \$58,200
39. Distributive Property **40.** Mike
41. $(-3.6, 14.4)$ **42.** $A(n) = 50 + 30(n - 1)$
43. Answers may vary. Sample: From 0 to 4 min, Luis biked away from his home. From 4 min to 6 min, Luis stopped biking. From 6 min to 9 min, Luis continued biking away from his home but at a higher speed than he traveled during the first 4 min. **44.** $x > -27.5$ and $x < 32.5$
45a. $f(x) = 1560x + 32,600$ **45b.** \$41,960

46. $34\dfrac{2}{3}$ ft **47a.** $y = 5x$

47b. Both intercepts are (0, 0).

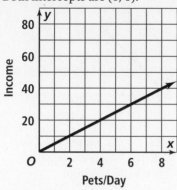

47c. 7 days **48.** $y = 3.5x$

49. 20% decrease **50.** The lines are parallel if they have the same slope; the lines are perpendicular if the lines are opposite reciprocals; the lines are neither parallel nor perpendicular if neither of the first two statements is true.

Final Test, Form G

1. $A = 6500 - 1100t$ **2.** $y = \frac{2}{3}x - 2$

3. no; 3 min late **4.** 6 days **5.** 9.54 ft **6.** 3.7 m/s

7. $5x^3 + 11x^2 - 5x - 4$ **8.** $\frac{9}{2}$ **9.** 3 or 1 **10.** 2

11.

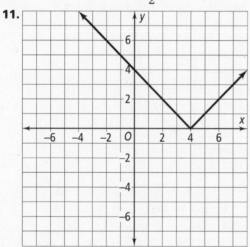

12. $\frac{4}{3}, -\frac{5}{2}$ **13.** $x - 3y = -5$ **14.** $4x - 5y = 20$

15. 5 **16.** 7 **17.** $(x + 9)(x - 3)$

18. $(2x + 1)(x^2 - 7)$ **19.** two **20.** -25

21. $6\sqrt{3}$ **22.** $15x^2\sqrt{x}$ **23.** $\frac{1}{12}$ **24.** $56x^5y^5$

25. $\frac{y^3z^3}{3x}$ **26.** $\frac{1}{2}$ **27.** 41%

28. $x \leq -6$

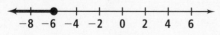

29. $x^3 + 3x^2 + 4x + 12$ **30.** 8 months
31. $0 \leq t \leq 5$ **32.** 3.75×10^5

33. $y \leq -x + 2$ **34.** $(11, -3)$ **35.** $(-2, -3), (1, 0)$

36. $y = 3x$ and $3x + 2y = 18$; book: $2.00; CD: $6.00
37. 400 **38.** $15,544 **39.** 623 books
40. The graph is shifted left 5 units and up 5 units.
41. $x + (x + 1) + (x + 2) = 219$; 72, 73, 74
42. $53.24 \leq 26.99 + 0.07x \leq 132$; 375 to
1500 minutes **43.** No, $10^2 + 18^2 \neq 22^2$.
44. $\frac{2(x - 1)}{x + 3}$ **45.** $3x^3 + 2x^2 + 4 + \frac{x + 1}{2x^2 - 3}$

46. $y = \frac{8}{15}x$ **47.** $xy = 120$ **48.** $r = \sqrt{G\frac{m_1m_2}{F_g}}$

49. 0.25%

50. $-1.6, 1.6$;

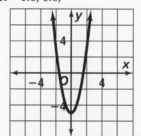

Quarter 1 Test, Form K

1. $3n - 2$ **2.** $A(n) = 2n$ **3.** $0 \leq t \leq 10$

4. 10, 25, 40 **5.** $\{2, 3, 4\}$ **6.** $\frac{6}{7}$ **7.** $54

8. $h = 2d$, where h represents height and d represents day **9.** 4 **10.** Associative Property of Multiplication **11.** $x < 42$ **12.** $x \geq -10$ **13.** 2 in.
14. 4 **15.** Distributive Property **16.** $72 = 24p$;
3 pencils **17.** yes **18.** 0 **19.** 7 **20.** $w = 3$ **21.** $t = 1$

22. $x = 1$ **23.** $\frac{20}{3y^8}$ **24.** 30 mi **25.** $x = 4.5$

Quarter 2 Test, Form K

1. $(1, 2)$

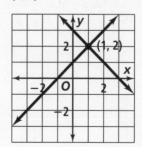

2.
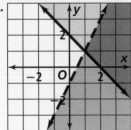

20.
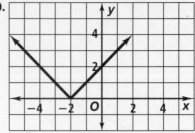

3. $(-2, 5)$ **4.** $m + h = 12$; $1.5h + 2m = 21.5$;
5 hamburgers, 7 milkshakes **5.** $d + n = 7$;
$0.1d + 0.05n = 0.55$; 4 dimes, 3 nickels

21. $m = 2$; $y = 2x - 1$ **22.** perpendicular
23. yes; $8 \geq 7$ **24.** The slopes are equal.
25. $y = 900 + 42x$; $3.00 per book

6.
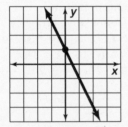

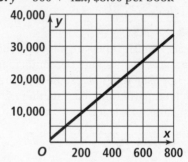

7.

x	$f(x) = -2x + 1$	(x, y)
-1	$f(x) = -2(-1) + 1$	$(-1, 3)$
0	$f(x) = -2(0) + 1$	$(0, 1)$
1	$f(x) = -2(1) + 1$	$(1, -1)$

Quarter 3 Test, Form K

1. $\dfrac{x^3}{y^2}$ **2.** $12x^5y$ **3.** 7.402×10^6

4. 2.36×10^2, 2.36×10^3, 23.6×10^3 **5.** $3, 6, 12$

6.
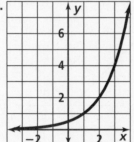

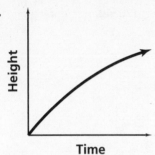

8. $y = 318 - 23x$; 249 **9.** $y + 4 = -3(x - 1)$
10. $f(x) = 20l$, where l represents the number of
lawns **11.** $m(x) = 8 - 0.25x$ **12.** $y = -2x$
13. $3; 5, 8$ **14.** $12; 69, 81$ **15.** $y = 2x + 3$ **16.** -1
17. $(3, 0); (0, 3)$ **18.** 50
19. negative correlation

7. $2, 6$ **8.** ± 4 **9.** $y = 2^x$; exponential **10.** $5\sqrt{3}$ ft
11. 9 **12.** $(3, -5)$ **13.** two real solutions
14. $-2x^2 - 11x + 2$ **15.** $24x^4 - 40x^2$
16. $y = x^2 + 10x + 24$; $(0, 24)$ **17.** $(x + 11)(x + 1)$
$x = -1$ and $x = -11$
18. $T = 20s^2$ **19.** $y = 3 \cdot 10^x$ **20.** 6

21.
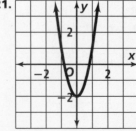

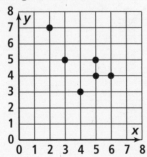

22a.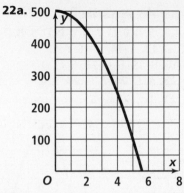

22b. 5.6 s **23.** exponential decay **24.** $(-1, 1)$ and $(-2, 4)$ **25.** shift left two units

Quarter 4 Test, Form K

1. $\frac{3}{8}$ **2.** $\frac{1}{28}$ **3.** 87

4.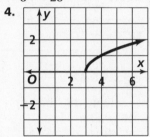

5. $T(x) = 1.5x$

6. 28% or $\frac{7}{25}$ **7.** inverse; The time decreases as the number of volunteers increases. **8.** minimum = 70; first quartile = 73; median = 80; third quartile = 85; maximum = 92 **9.** 24

10. 5 **11.** $\frac{\sqrt{5} - \sqrt{3}}{2}$ **12.** $4n\sqrt{2n}$ **13.** $\frac{1}{4}$ **14.** 6, 1

15. $x = 1$;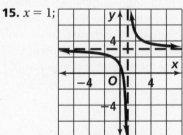

16. The graph will be the same shape, but it will move down 3 units. **17.** $\frac{1}{4}$ **18.** $x^2 + 3x + 5$

19. $\frac{x^2 - 3x + 2}{x^2 - 9}$ **20.** 64.3 ft **21.** -2

22. $\frac{5}{10}$ or $\frac{1}{2}$ **23.** mode **24.** 30

25. a. Dependent b. Independent

Mid-Course Test, Form K

1. 40 mph **2.** 0.5% **3.** $h = A/b$ **4.** 4 **5.** 10
6. The area will be multiplied by 9. **7.** 25
8. 4 **9.** 2 **10.** $y > 2$ **11.** $1 < x < 4$
12. $x < 6$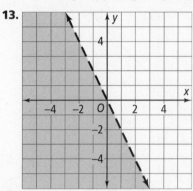

13.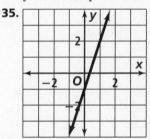

14. $x \geq 4$ **15.** $\{0, 2, 8\}$ **16.** 128, 141 **17.** yes; $6 \geq -2$ **18.** infinitely many solutions **19.** $61
20. 0.25 gal **21.** $7 **22.** $P = 4x + 14$; $x = 2$
23. $T \leq 2x$ **24.** $x = 0.25(80)$; 20
25. $0.85(300) = x$; 255 **26.** 54.2% **27.** $\frac{1}{2}$ **28.** 6
29. $y = 2x$ **30.** $x = 5$ **31.** 5 **32.** $y = 3x$
33. $y = x^2$ **34.** positive weak correlation

35.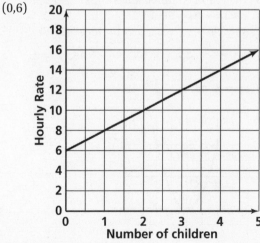

36. 3 units up; The point $(0, 0)$ becomes $(0, 3)$ with the new equation. **37.** 6 ft **38.** $60 **39.** Distributive Property **40.** Brand B **41.** $(2, 12)$ **42.** $\{1, 2, 3, 4, 6, 8\}$ **43.** The speed of the object is zero. **44.** $-4 < x < 4$ **45.** $f(x) = 5x + 50$ **46.** 6 **47.** $y = 2x + 6$; $(0, 6)$

48. $y = 2x$ **49.** 50% increase **50.** The lines are perpendicular.

Final Test, Form K

1. $A = 650 - 100t$ **2.** 6.93 ft **3.** 62 mi/h **4.** 15 h
5. 6.93 ft **6.** 4.2 m/s **7.** $x^2 + 5x + 8$ **8.** 7
9. 4 or -1 **10.** 2

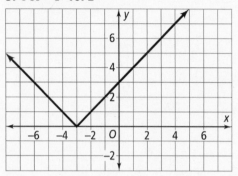

12. $-2, -4$ **13.** $-3x + y = -2$ **14.** $3x + 4y = -12$
15. 11 **16.** 32 **17.** $(x + 6)(x + 2)$
18. $(x + 3)(x + 2)$ **19.** two **20.** 16, 20 **21.** $3\sqrt{2}$
22. $4x^2$ **23.** $\dfrac{1}{4}$ **24.** $8x^5$ **25.** $3xy^4$ **26.** $\dfrac{1}{2}$
27. $\dfrac{13}{50}$ or 26%
28. $x < 5$

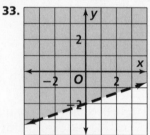

29. $x^3 + 2x^2 + x + 2$ **30.** 5 months
31. $0 \le m \le 5$ **32.** 4.5×10^4
33.

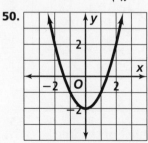

34. $(5, 2)$ **35.** $(3, 5)$ **36.** 16 cars and 8 trucks **37.**
5 **38.** $32.40 **39.** 7 months
40. The graph is shifted left 2 units.
41. $x + (x + 2) = 30; 14, 16$
42. $37 \le 25 + 2x \le 53$; 6 to 14 rides **43.** 20
44. $\dfrac{1}{6(x + 3)}$ **45.** $x + 3 + \dfrac{2}{x + 1}$ **46.** $y = 2x$
47. $xy = 8$ **48.** $r = \sqrt{\dfrac{A}{\pi}}$ **49.** 4%
50.

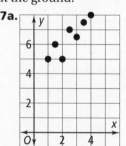

End-of-Course Assessment

1. A, D **2.** D **3.** B **4.** A **5.** B **6.** D **7.** A, B **8.** D **9.** B, D
10. A **11.** B **12.** C, D **13.** A **14.** B **15.** A, C
16. A, B, C **17.** A **18.** B **19.** B, C **20.** B, C, D
21. B, D **22.** C, D **23.** A, D **24.** E, G **25.** A, C
26. $x = \dfrac{7}{2} = 3.5$ **27.** $3x^2 - 5x - 3$

28. 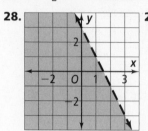 **29.**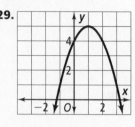

30. The mean and median will increase, and the range will stay the same. There is no mode.
31. $x = -4$ and $x = 8$ **32.** $5°, 35°,$ and $140°$ **33.** $(1, 5)$
34. $C = 20 - 3.99x$. **35.** $y = -x + 8$ **36.** 225 m^2
37. positive correlation **38.** about 63,000
39. $6700 per month **40.** Answers may vary.
Sample: 2, 2, 2, 2, ... **41.** $y = x + 6$ **42.** $2\dfrac{7}{12}$
43. 0.437 **44.** -0.0075 m per hour **45.** The graph is translated 1 unit down. **46.** $y > 5x - 1$
47. $(3, 11)$ **48.** $7x$ **49.** 1.706 **50.** $(-2, -9)$
51. $x = 4$ **52.** The domain value 300 is mapped to two range values. The relation is not a function.
53. $a_n = \dfrac{2}{3} + (n - 1)\dfrac{1}{12}$ **54.** There is a negative correlation and also a causal relationship. As the cost per pound of salad goes down, the amount of salad sold will go up. **55.** The account grew by an average of $103.33 per month. **56a.** 2 seconds. **56b.** The domain is all nonnegative real numbers less than about 4.43. Negative numbers do not make sense in this situation because time cannot be negative. Numbers greater than 4.43 do not make sense, because they are after the ball would hit the ground.
57a.

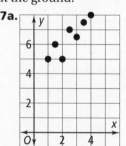

57b. Answers may vary. Sample: $y = x + 4$

58a. about 65 people

58b. Both x and y must be nonnegative numbers. As the number of attending family members increases, the cost per person decreases. The cost per person will eventually approach $3.50.

59a. 4.6; the slope tells you that girls from ages 2–7 gain about 4.6 lbs per year. **59b.** 0.992; the correlation coefficient is close to 1 so there is a strong positive correlation between the age and weight of girls from ages 2–7.

60a. $x = -3.73$ or $x = -0.27$ OR $x = -2 \pm \sqrt{3}$

60b. The solutions are irrational, which are difficult to graph or factor. **61a.** Yes, the values in the table represent a function. Each domain value is mapped to exactly one range value.

61b. $6 per pound; 90 lb **62a.** The student is incorrect. The solutions are $x = 8$ and $x = -3$

62b.

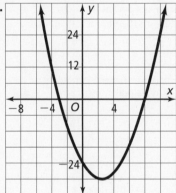

63a. $f(x) = 35 + 0.05x$, where x is the number of minutes of use each month. The domain is all nonnegative real numbers, the range is all numbers greater than or equal to 35.

63b. about $52.28 **64a.** $2\pi(x^2 - 2x + 1) + 2\pi(2x^2 - 2x) = 2\pi(3x^2 - 4x + 1)$ **64b.** 640π **65a.** There is no solution to the system. **65b.** If you solve both equations for y, you find that both graphs have a slope of $-\dfrac{7}{2}$, but they have different y-intercepts which means the lines are parallel and do not intersect.

Performance Task 1 Scoring Rubric

Choosing a Movie-Rental Plan

The Scoring Rubric proposes a maximum number of points for each of the parts that make up the Performance Task. The maximum number of points is based on the complexity and difficulty level of the sub-task. For some parts, you may decide to award partial credit to students who may have shown some understanding of the concepts assessed, but may not have responded fully or correctly to the question posed.

Task Parts	Maximum Points
a. $A(x) = 1.50x$; $B(x) = 10$; $C(x) = 5 + 2x$	2
b. It makes sense to choose Plan B over Plan A only if you rent 7 or more movies per month. Note that $A(1) = \$1.50$ while $B(1) = \$10$, $A(2) = \$1.50(2) = \$3$ while $B(2) = \$10$, etc. Plan A is less expensive until you rent 7 movies: $A(7) = \$1.50(7) = \$10.50$ while $B(7) = \$10$, $A(8) = \$1.50(8) = \$12$ while $B(8) = \$10$, etc.	4
c. It makes sense to choose Plan C over Plan B only if you rent 2 or fewer movies per month. Note that $C(0) = \$5 + \$2(0) = \$5$ while $B(0) = \$10$; also $C(1) = \$5 + \$2(1) = \$7$ while $B(0) = \$10$; also $C(2) = \$5 + \$2(2) = \$9$ while $B(2) = \$10$. So Plan C is less expensive until you rent 3 movies: $C(3) = \$5 + \$2(3) = \$11$ while $B(3) = \$10$.	4
d. Plan A is always more cost-effective than Plan C, because each movie costs \$1.50 rather than \$2. This does not mean that Plan A is a better choice than Plan C for everyone, because someone might value convenience and selection more than cost.	4
e. Sample Answer: I would choose Plan A, because I rent only a few movies per year. The cost is the least with this plan, and there would be plenty of selection for me.	4
Total points	18

Performance Task 2 Scoring Rubric

Expanding a Parking Lot

The Scoring Rubric proposes a maximum number of points for each of the parts that make up the Performance Task. The maximum number of points is based on the complexity and difficulty level of the sub-task. For some parts, you may decide to award partial credit to students who may have shown some understanding of the concepts assessed, but may not have responded fully or correctly to the question posed.

Task Parts	Maximum Points
a. Check students' drawings. The original parking lot is a rectangle with length 600 ft and width 400 ft. The expanded parking lot is a bigger rectangle with length $(600 + x)$ ft and width $(400 + x)$ ft.	2
b. The area of the original parking lot is $600(400) = 240,000$ ft^2. Since they want to double the area of the parking lot, the area of the expanded parking lot will be $2(240,000) = 480,000$ ft^2. So an equation to solve is $(600 + x)(400 + x) = 480,000$. Steps for solving this equation: $240,000 + 1000x + x^2 = 480,000$; $x^2 + 1000x - 240,000 = 0$; $(x + 1200)(x - 200) = 0$; $x = -1200$ ft or $x = 200$ ft. Use only the positive value: $x = 200$ ft.	4
c. The area of the new portion of the parking lot is 240,000 ft^2. The length of the new parking lot is $600 + 200 = 800$ ft, and the width of the new parking lot is $400 + 200 = 600$ ft. So the perimeter of the new parking lot is $2(800 + 600) = 2800$ ft.	4
d. The cost to double the area of the lot is $\$2(240,000) = \$480,000$. The cost to fence the lot is $\$30(2800) = \$84,000$. The total cost is $\$480,000 + \$84,000 = \$564,000$.	4
e. The amount of money to be raised is half the total cost, or $0.5(\$564,000) = \$282,000$. Since $100(\$200) + 2620(\$100) = \$282,000$, one possible solution is for 100 faculty to buy a sticker and for 2620 students to buy a sticker. There are many possible solutions to this problem.	4
Total Points	18

Performance Task 3 Scoring Rubric

Projectile Motion

The Scoring Rubric proposes a maximum number of points for each of the parts that make up the Performance Task. The maximum number of points is based on the complexity and difficulty level of the sub-task. For some parts, you may decide to award partial credit to students who may have shown some understanding of the concepts assessed, but may not have responded fully or correctly to the question posed.

Task Parts	Maximum Points
a. Write the equation using $y_0 = 6$ and $v = 50$: $y = \left(-\dfrac{32}{50^2}\right)x^2 + x + 6$. Check students' graphs of this equation. When $x = 100$, $y = \left(-\dfrac{32}{50^2}\right)(100)^2 + 100 + 6 = -22$. So the ball does not land in the friend's glove because she is at $y = 5$, not $y = -22$.	4
b. If the friend catches the ball, then $y = 5$. The point that must lie on the graph of the ball's path is about $(79, 5)$.	2
c. Write the equation using $x = 100$ and $y = 5$: $5 = \left(-\dfrac{32}{v^2}\right)(100)^2 + 100 + y_0$, or $y_0 = \left(\dfrac{32}{v^2}\right)(100)^2 - 95$. There are many possible ordered pairs (v, y_0) that are solutions to this equation, which you can see by graphing.	4
d. One possible solution is for initial height y_0 to be 6 ft and initial velocity v to be about 56.3 ft/sec. Check this in the original equation: $y = \left(-\dfrac{32}{56.3^2}\right)(100)^2 + 100 + 6 \approx 5$ ft. Since the friend is holding a glove at 5 ft, she will catch the ball.	4
Total Points	14

Performance Task 4 Scoring Rubric

Calculating Inflation

The Scoring Rubric proposes a maximum number of points for each of the parts that make up the Performance Task. The maximum number of points is based on the complexity and difficulty level of the sub-task. For some parts, you may decide to award partial credit to students who may have shown some understanding of the concepts assessed, but may not have responded fully or correctly to the question posed.

Task Parts	Maximum Points
a. Bread: $r = \left(\dfrac{1.39}{0.99}\right)^{\frac{1}{9}} - 1 \approx 3.8\%$. Butter: $r = \left(\dfrac{2.67}{2.80}\right)^{\frac{1}{9}} - 1 \approx -0.5\%$. Eggs: $r = \left(\dfrac{1.77}{0.96}\right)^{\frac{1}{9}} - 1 \approx 7.0\%$. Ground beef: $r = \left(\dfrac{2.19}{1.63}\right)^{\frac{1}{9}} - 1 \approx 3.3\%$. Oranges: $r = \left(\dfrac{0.93}{0.62}\right)^{\frac{1}{9}} - 1 \approx 4.6\%$. Tomatoes: $r = \left(\dfrac{1.96}{1.57}\right)^{\frac{1}{9}} - 1 \approx 2.5\%$. Cheddar cheese: $r = \left(\dfrac{4.55}{3.76}\right)^{\frac{1}{9}} - 1 \approx 2.1\%$. Peanut butter: $r = \left(\dfrac{2.10}{1.66}\right)^{\frac{1}{9}} - 1 \approx 0.8\%$. Meat cutlets: $r = \left(\dfrac{3.29}{3.46}\right)^{\frac{1}{9}} - 1 \approx -0.6\%$.	5
b. The food that had the lowest inflation rate was meat cutlets. The food that had the greatest inflation rate was eggs.	2
c. The foods that had negative annual inflation rates were butter and meat cutlets. A negative annual inflation rate means that prices decreased.	2
d. No, it does not make sense to add the percentages of each item to determine the inflation rate for a basket of groceries. The sum of the percentages is 23%.	2
e. This basket of groceries cost $17.75 in 2000 and $20.85 in 2009. Find the inflation rate using these two costs: $r = \left(\dfrac{20.85}{17.75}\right)^{\frac{1}{9}} - 1 \approx 1.8\%$.	3
f. Use the annual inflation rate of 1.8%, and apply it for 6 more years (since $2015 - 2009 = 6$ years). Predicted cost $= \$20.85(1.018)^6 = \$23.21$.	4
Total Points	18

Multiple Choice

1. C
2. D
3. D
4. D
5. C
6. E
7. B
8. A
9. D
10. E
11. E

12. A
13. D
14. C
15. B
16. D
17. C
18. A
19. D
20. C
21. D
22. E

23. A
24. B
25. B
26. E
27. D
28. D
29. A
30. E
31. D
32. E

Student-Produced Responses

1. 12
2. 8
3. 56
4. 0
5. 7
6. 400
7. .4
8. 10
9. 62
10. .034

Note: 12 is also a correct response for problem 8.

1.	Ⓐ	Ⓑ	Ⓒ	Ⓓ
2.	Ⓕ	Ⓖ	Ⓗ	Ⓙ
3.	Ⓐ	Ⓑ	Ⓒ	Ⓓ
4.	Ⓕ	Ⓖ	Ⓗ	Ⓙ
5.	Ⓐ	Ⓑ	Ⓒ	Ⓓ
6.	Ⓕ	Ⓖ	Ⓗ	Ⓙ
7.	Ⓐ	Ⓑ	Ⓒ	Ⓓ
8.	Ⓕ	Ⓖ	Ⓗ	Ⓙ
9.	Ⓐ	Ⓑ	Ⓒ	Ⓓ
10.	Ⓕ	Ⓖ	Ⓗ	Ⓙ
11.	Ⓐ	Ⓑ	Ⓒ	Ⓓ
12.	Ⓕ	Ⓖ	Ⓗ	Ⓙ
13.	Ⓐ	Ⓑ	Ⓒ	Ⓓ
14.	Ⓕ	Ⓖ	Ⓗ	Ⓙ
15.	Ⓐ	Ⓑ	Ⓒ	Ⓓ
16.	Ⓕ	Ⓖ	Ⓗ	Ⓙ
17.	Ⓐ	Ⓑ	Ⓒ	Ⓓ
18.	Ⓕ	Ⓖ	Ⓗ	Ⓙ
19.	Ⓐ	Ⓑ	Ⓒ	Ⓓ
20.	Ⓕ	Ⓖ	Ⓗ	Ⓙ
21.	Ⓐ	Ⓑ	Ⓒ	Ⓓ
22.	Ⓕ	Ⓖ	Ⓗ	Ⓙ
23.	Ⓐ	Ⓑ	Ⓒ	Ⓓ
24.	Ⓕ	Ⓖ	Ⓗ	Ⓙ
25.	Ⓐ	Ⓑ	Ⓒ	Ⓓ
26.	Ⓕ	Ⓖ	Ⓗ	Ⓙ
27.	Ⓐ	Ⓑ	Ⓒ	Ⓓ
28.	Ⓕ	Ⓖ	Ⓗ	Ⓙ

29.	Ⓐ	Ⓑ	Ⓒ	Ⓓ
30.	Ⓕ	Ⓖ	Ⓗ	Ⓙ
31.	Ⓐ	Ⓑ	Ⓒ	Ⓓ
32.	Ⓕ	Ⓖ	Ⓗ	Ⓙ
33.	Ⓐ	Ⓑ	Ⓒ	Ⓓ
34.	Ⓕ	Ⓖ	Ⓗ	Ⓙ
35.	Ⓐ	Ⓑ	Ⓒ	Ⓓ
36.	Ⓕ	Ⓖ	Ⓗ	Ⓙ
37.	Ⓐ	Ⓑ	Ⓒ	Ⓓ
38.	Ⓕ	Ⓖ	Ⓗ	Ⓙ
39.	Ⓐ	Ⓑ	Ⓒ	Ⓓ
40.	Ⓕ	Ⓖ	Ⓗ	Ⓙ
41.	Ⓐ	Ⓑ	Ⓒ	Ⓓ
42.	Ⓕ	Ⓖ	Ⓗ	Ⓙ
43.	Ⓐ	Ⓑ	Ⓒ	Ⓓ
44.	Ⓕ	Ⓖ	Ⓗ	Ⓙ
45.	Ⓐ	Ⓑ	Ⓒ	Ⓓ
46.	Ⓕ	Ⓖ	Ⓗ	Ⓙ
47.	Ⓐ	Ⓑ	Ⓒ	Ⓓ
48.	Ⓕ	Ⓖ	Ⓗ	Ⓙ
49.	Ⓐ	Ⓑ	Ⓒ	Ⓓ
50.	Ⓕ	Ⓖ	Ⓗ	Ⓙ
51.	Ⓐ	Ⓑ	Ⓒ	Ⓓ
52.	Ⓕ	Ⓖ	Ⓗ	Ⓙ
53.	Ⓐ	Ⓑ	Ⓒ	Ⓓ
54.	Ⓕ	Ⓖ	Ⓗ	Ⓙ
55.	Ⓐ	Ⓑ	Ⓒ	Ⓓ
56.	Ⓕ	Ⓖ	Ⓗ	Ⓙ

1.	Ⓐ	Ⓑ	Ⓒ	Ⓓ		29.	Ⓐ	Ⓑ	Ⓒ	Ⓓ
2.	Ⓕ	Ⓖ	Ⓗ	Ⓙ		30.	Ⓕ	Ⓖ	Ⓗ	Ⓙ
3.	Ⓐ	Ⓑ	Ⓒ	Ⓓ		31.	Ⓐ	Ⓑ	Ⓒ	Ⓓ
4.	Ⓕ	Ⓖ	Ⓗ	Ⓙ		32.	Ⓕ	Ⓖ	Ⓗ	Ⓙ
5.	Ⓐ	Ⓑ	Ⓒ	Ⓓ		33.	Ⓐ	Ⓑ	Ⓒ	Ⓓ
6.	Ⓕ	Ⓖ	Ⓗ	Ⓙ		34.	Ⓕ	Ⓖ	Ⓗ	Ⓙ
7.	Ⓐ	Ⓑ	Ⓒ	Ⓓ		35.	Ⓐ	Ⓑ	Ⓒ	Ⓓ
8.	Ⓕ	Ⓖ	Ⓗ	Ⓙ		36.	Ⓕ	Ⓖ	Ⓗ	Ⓙ
9.	Ⓐ	Ⓑ	Ⓒ	Ⓓ		37.	Ⓐ	Ⓑ	Ⓒ	Ⓓ
10.	Ⓕ	Ⓖ	Ⓗ	Ⓙ		38.	Ⓕ	Ⓖ	Ⓗ	Ⓙ
11.	Ⓐ	Ⓑ	Ⓒ	Ⓓ		39.	Ⓐ	Ⓑ	Ⓒ	Ⓓ
12.	Ⓕ	Ⓖ	Ⓗ	Ⓙ		40.	Ⓕ	Ⓖ	Ⓗ	Ⓙ
13.	Ⓐ	Ⓑ	Ⓒ	Ⓓ		41.	Ⓐ	Ⓑ	Ⓒ	Ⓓ
14.	Ⓕ	Ⓖ	Ⓗ	Ⓙ		42.	Ⓕ	Ⓖ	Ⓗ	Ⓙ
15.	Ⓐ	Ⓑ	Ⓒ	Ⓓ		43.	Ⓐ	Ⓑ	Ⓒ	Ⓓ
16.	Ⓕ	Ⓖ	Ⓗ	Ⓙ		44.	Ⓕ	Ⓖ	Ⓗ	Ⓙ
17.	Ⓐ	Ⓑ	Ⓒ	Ⓓ		45.	Ⓐ	Ⓑ	Ⓒ	Ⓓ
18.	Ⓕ	Ⓖ	Ⓗ	Ⓙ		46.	Ⓕ	Ⓖ	Ⓗ	Ⓙ
19.	Ⓐ	Ⓑ	Ⓒ	Ⓓ		47.	Ⓐ	Ⓑ	Ⓒ	Ⓓ
20.	Ⓕ	Ⓖ	Ⓗ	Ⓙ		48.	Ⓕ	Ⓖ	Ⓗ	Ⓙ
21.	Ⓐ	Ⓑ	Ⓒ	Ⓓ		49.	Ⓐ	Ⓑ	Ⓒ	Ⓓ
22.	Ⓕ	Ⓖ	Ⓗ	Ⓙ		50.	Ⓕ	Ⓖ	Ⓗ	Ⓙ
23.	Ⓐ	Ⓑ	Ⓒ	Ⓓ		51.	Ⓐ	Ⓑ	Ⓒ	Ⓓ
24.	Ⓕ	Ⓖ	Ⓗ	Ⓙ		52.	Ⓕ	Ⓖ	Ⓗ	Ⓙ
25.	Ⓐ	Ⓑ	Ⓒ	Ⓓ		53.	Ⓐ	Ⓑ	Ⓒ	Ⓓ
26.	Ⓕ	Ⓖ	Ⓗ	Ⓙ		54.	Ⓕ	Ⓖ	Ⓗ	Ⓙ
27.	Ⓐ	Ⓑ	Ⓒ	Ⓓ		55.	Ⓐ	Ⓑ	Ⓒ	Ⓓ
28.	Ⓕ	Ⓖ	Ⓗ	Ⓙ		56.	Ⓕ	Ⓖ	Ⓗ	Ⓙ

1. 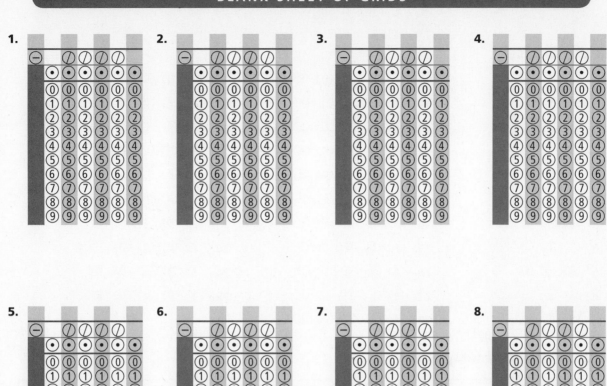 **2.** **3.** **4.**

5. 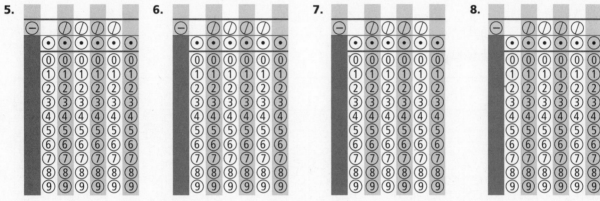 **6.** **7.** **8.**

9. 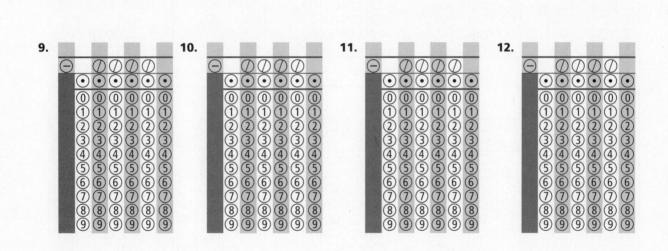 **10.** **11.** **12.**

Multiple Choice

1. Ⓐ Ⓑ Ⓒ Ⓓ Ⓔ
2. Ⓐ Ⓑ Ⓒ Ⓓ Ⓔ
3. Ⓐ Ⓑ Ⓒ Ⓓ Ⓔ
4. Ⓐ Ⓑ Ⓒ Ⓓ Ⓔ
5. Ⓐ Ⓑ Ⓒ Ⓓ Ⓔ
6. Ⓐ Ⓑ Ⓒ Ⓓ Ⓔ
7. Ⓐ Ⓑ Ⓒ Ⓓ Ⓔ
8. Ⓐ Ⓑ Ⓒ Ⓓ Ⓔ
9. Ⓐ Ⓑ Ⓒ Ⓓ Ⓔ
10. Ⓐ Ⓑ Ⓒ Ⓓ Ⓔ
11. Ⓐ Ⓑ Ⓒ Ⓓ Ⓔ

12. Ⓐ Ⓑ Ⓒ Ⓓ Ⓔ
13. Ⓐ Ⓑ Ⓒ Ⓓ Ⓔ
14. Ⓐ Ⓑ Ⓒ Ⓓ Ⓔ
15. Ⓐ Ⓑ Ⓒ Ⓓ Ⓔ
16. Ⓐ Ⓑ Ⓒ Ⓓ Ⓔ
17. Ⓐ Ⓑ Ⓒ Ⓓ Ⓔ
18. Ⓐ Ⓑ Ⓒ Ⓓ Ⓔ
19. Ⓐ Ⓑ Ⓒ Ⓓ Ⓔ
20. Ⓐ Ⓑ Ⓒ Ⓓ Ⓔ
21. Ⓐ Ⓑ Ⓒ Ⓓ Ⓔ
22. Ⓐ Ⓑ Ⓒ Ⓓ Ⓔ

23. Ⓐ Ⓑ Ⓒ Ⓓ Ⓔ
24. Ⓐ Ⓑ Ⓒ Ⓓ Ⓔ
25. Ⓐ Ⓑ Ⓒ Ⓓ Ⓔ
26. Ⓐ Ⓑ Ⓒ Ⓓ Ⓔ
27. Ⓐ Ⓑ Ⓒ Ⓓ Ⓔ
28. Ⓐ Ⓑ Ⓒ Ⓓ Ⓔ
29. Ⓐ Ⓑ Ⓒ Ⓓ Ⓔ
30. Ⓐ Ⓑ Ⓒ Ⓓ Ⓔ
31. Ⓐ Ⓑ Ⓒ Ⓓ Ⓔ
32. Ⓐ Ⓑ Ⓒ Ⓓ Ⓔ

Student-Produced Responses